SIMPLE

WOODEN

TOYS

SIMPLE WOODEN TOYS

RON FULLER
& CATHY MEEUS

HEADLINE

A Quarto Book

Copyright © 1995 Quarto Publishing plc

First published in Great Britain in 1995
by HEADLINE BOOK PUBLISHING

HEADLINE BOOK PUBLISHING
A division of Hodder Headline PLC
338 Euston Road
London NW1 3BH

British Library Cataloguing in Publication Data

Fuller, Ron
 Simple Wooden Toys
 I. Title
 745.592
 ISBN 0-7472-1288-0

Designed and produced by
Quarto Publishing plc
The Old Brewery
6 Blundell Street
London N7 9BH

Senior editor **Maria Morgan**
Senior art editor **Mark Stevens**
Designer **John Grain**
Illustrators **Kuo Kang Chen, Carol Hill, David
Kemp** (plans)
Photographers **Colin Bowling, Paul Forrester,
Laura Wickenden**
Art director **Moira Clinch**
Editorial director **Sophie Collins**

Typeset by Genesis Typesetting, Rochester, Kent
Manufactured in Hong Kong by Regent
Publishing Services Ltd
Printed in China by Leefung-Asco Printers Ltd

Publisher's note:
Woodworking can be dangerous. Both
hand and power tools can quickly sever
nerves, tendons or limbs. Always exercise
extreme caution when working with wood.
Always read tool instruction manuals, use
the safety guards provided, and wear
protective gear and clothing. For illustrative
purposes, many of these steps were
omitted, but this is not recommended
operating procedure.
  As far as the methods and techniques
mentioned in this book are concerned, all
statements, information and advice given
are believed to be true and accurate.
However, neither the authors, copyright
holder nor the publisher can accept any
legal liability for errors or omissions.

CONTENTS

General note on metric and imperial sizing

The instructions in this book give the metric size first followed by the imperial equivalent. When referring to a measured distance, this is a simple mathematical conversion. However, when referring to wood thicknesses and sizes of drill bits, for example, the imperial measurement refers to the dimensions of the nearest equivalent product available. For this reason, it may not be a precise conversion. When working on a project in this book always use either metric or imperial measurements to avoid problems.

· INTRODUCTION ·

Wood is a remarkable material with a special feel and quality. In this age of plastic and electronics, traditional wooden toys are a rare treat. Wooden toys are fun to make and it is always very rewarding to watch children enjoying toys made specially for them. All the projects in this book are original designs based on traditional styles, and are made by professional toy-makers. The ideas and techniques may vary from maker to maker, but the results are always stunning.

Whether you are a complete woodworking novice or a skilled craftsperson, the clear and concise illustrated step-by-step instructions will allow you to develop and improve your skills. The first part of the book outlines the materials, tools and equipment you will need and takes you through the basic techniques used in the projects. A basic tool-kit found in most households is really all you need, and this lively assortment of colourful toys, puzzles and moving figures is guaranteed to inspire and encourage you. Work your way through the book, or choose projects to suit your family and friends.

· HOW TO USE THIS BOOK ·

The first part of the book deals with materials and equipment and basic techniques used in the projects. The basic principles needed to make the toys are illustrated and include: scaling up and transferring designs; choosing and using wood and other materials; cutting and drilling; gluing; painting and varnishing. There are then 19 projects to make, presented in the following format.

EQUIPMENT

Fretsaw

Tenon saw

Glasspaper

Drill and bits
4mm (⅛in), 5mm (³⁄₁₆in), 9mm (⅜in) flat bit

Round file (optional)

Pair of compasses

All component parts are listed by number, name and type of material for easy reference.

The first spread includes a photograph, a brief introduction to the toy and the specific materials and equipment needed to make it.

The spread also gives complete templates and plans for the project, including the scale where not shown full size.

Stage One

The positioning of the components is shown in a unique "exploded" photograph, with numbers corresponding to the parts list. While coloured here, check

which parts are actually painted before assembly.

Stage Two

These are the fully illustrated step-by-step instructions for making the project.

The final page shows a large, full-colour photograph of the finished toy.

Stage Three

·EQUIPMENT AND MATERIALS·

The projects in this book can be undertaken by anyone with a basic knowledge of woodworking. They require a minimum of tools and equipment, and the materials are all readily available from hardware stores and modelmaker's suppliers.

EQUIPMENT

The largest item you will need is a sturdy workbench. A purpose-made wooden bench is ideal. However, a portable workbench of the type used for D-I-Y work in the home, is perfectly adequate. It is important to have a good quality woodworking vice with wooden jaws. If you have one with metal jaws, you can adapt it by screwing two pieces of 12mm (½in) plywood to the inside of the vice. A bench hook is useful for steadying items that cannot be held in a vice.

The tools and equipment you need in addition to your workbench and vice are listed at the start of each project. The list on the right summarizes the items common to most projects. The most essential tools are indicated with a bullet • The emphasis is on simple hand tools, but if you have more sophisticated power tools, these can, of course, be used.

BASIC TOOL KIT

- • Tenon saw
- • Fretsaw and mount
  (cutting table)
- Coping saw
- Hacksaw
- Junior hacksaw
- Chisels
  12mm (½in) and 6mm (¼in)
- • Craft knife
- • Smoothing plane
- • Block plane
- • Small hammer
- • Mallet
- Rasp
- Glasspaper
- Flat and round metal files
- Ordinary pliers
- • Round-nosed pliers

- Needle-nosed pliers
- Diagonal cutters
- Tin snips
- • Screwdrivers
  (slotted and cross-head)
- • Power drill and pillar stand
- • Selection of high-speed and flat bits
- Countersink bit
- • Pin chuck
- Hole saws
- • G-clamps
- • Long ruler
- Set square
- Soldering iron and multicore solder
- Scissors
- Protractor
- Compasses

WOOD AND DOWEL

Plywood

Plywood made from thin layers of timber is one of the main materials for the maker of wooden toys. Birch plywood from Finland or Russia is the most commonly used, although Ramin and Far East plywood are used for some projects. Always choose the best quality available – grade BB – in which both sides are smooth and knot-free.

Plywood is available in a variety of thicknesses. For the projects in this book the metric sizes used are 3mm, 4mm, 6.5mm, 9mm, and 12mm. The traditional imperial measurements are respectively ⅛in (for 3 and 4mm), ¼in, ⅜in and ½in.

Aero ply

Available in 1.8mm (¹⁄₁₆in) thickness, this is a flexible plywood used extensively for model-making and is available from modelmaker's suppliers.

Softwood

Usually pine, this easily obtainable category of wood is used in many projects in this book where a solid piece of timber is required. Select wood that is knot-free and that has a consistent close grain. Beech, the traditional material used by German toymakers can be substituted, but it is more expensive and sometimes hard to find outside specialist timber merchants.

Equipment

1 Needle-nosed pliers; **2** round-nosed pliers; **3** flat bit; **4** high-speed bits **5** countersink bit; **6** pin hammer; **7** G-clamp; **8** blades; **9** craft knife; **10** slotted screwdriver; **11** cross-head screwdriver; **12** tenon saw; **13** steel rule.

Plywood

1 Birch; **2** aircraft-grade plywood; **3** ramin; **4** mahogany; **5** plywood;

Softwood is sold in "nominal" sizes. This means that if you buy a length of planed all round (PAR) timber, the size you are actually given will be approximately 1.8mm ($\frac{1}{16}$in) smaller all round. The instructions in this book refer to the nominal size, but to save yourself the trouble of planing, always select PAR timber.

Dowel

Dowels are used extensively in toymaking for pivots, shafts and spacers. Where dowel is specified, birch is the preferred timber because it is easy to work with, has a pleasing appearance and is most easily obtained from modelmaker's suppliers and craft shops. Before buying check the dowel for roundness as sometimes faults in the cutting process create an oval or stepped section that could create a problem in making a toy. Ramin dowel is more difficult to work with and is therefore a less satisfactory alternative.

Dowels are available in a range of diameters. The usual sizes are 4mm ($\frac{1}{8}$in), 5mm ($\frac{3}{16}$in), 6.5mm ($\frac{1}{4}$in), 9mm ($\frac{3}{8}$in) and 12mm ($\frac{1}{2}$in). Like all wood measurements, the size you buy may not be completely accurate. It may therefore be necessary to adjust the dowel thickness by sanding, in order to ensure that it fits to the degree of tightness required. Similarly, if you cannot obtain the precise size you need, it may be possible to buy the next size up and sand down to fit.

Wood and dowel

1 Softwood; **2** pine; **3** beech; **4 5 6** dowels; **7** round dowel; **8** oval dowel; **9** irregular dowel.

Fixings

1 Screws; **2** panel pins; **3** gimp pins; **4** hooks and eyes; **5** PVA wood glue; **6** rapid-drying epoxy; **7** impact adhesive; **8** superglue.

FIXINGS

Screws

There is a huge variety of screw types to choose from, and selection is largely a matter of personal preference. They are available in different lengths and gauges (expressed as a numbered size) to fit different sizes of drilled holes. In this book, most of the screws used are countersunk, that is, they have a flat head that when inserted in a suitably drilled hole, will lie flush to the surface. Cross-head screws are usually easier to tighten. The newest screw designs, which have a dual thread that goes in more smoothly and grips more firmly, are generally preferable. Whatever type of screw you are using, it is important to use a compatible screwdriver with a good blade so as to avoid damage to the screw head which could spoil the appearance of the toy.

Panel pins and gimp pins

Panel pins of various sizes and gauges are often used to secure an assembly in addition to glue. They can be brass or steel. For toymaking, it is best to use the thinnest gauge available. Gimp pins are large-headed brass or mild steel pins used in upholstery. They are specified in some projects where a decorative effect is desired, but if you cannot obtain them, steel panel pins will serve the purpose just as well.

Glues

Four types of glue are used in the projects in this book.

PVA wood glue. This is a general-purpose glue that is applied only to one of the surfaces to be joined. Wipe away any excess with a damp cloth immediately. Choose the type that is fast-grab and quick-drying which can be obtained from modelmaker's suppliers. PVA wood glue can be thinned with an equal volume of water for gluing paper.

Rapid-drying epoxy glue. This is supplied in two parts – adhesive and hardener – that have to be mixed in equal parts before use. It has good filling properties and provides a strong bond for metal and wood.

Impact adhesive. Providing a strong and immediate bond, this glue should be applied to both surfaces and left for ten minutes before joining the parts.

Superglue. A useful adhesive for small parts that cannot easily be supported for long periods of drying, utmost care must be taken not to allow the glue to come into contact with skin or eyes.

Use fine synthetic watercolour brushes for all detail work. They are soft but durable and are available in a variety of sizes. Make sure that you only buy good quality brushes. For painting large areas, use a hoghair or synthetic oil-painting brush.

OTHER MATERIALS

Metal parts

Some toys use small metal parts in addition to the main wooden structure. Tin and brass sheet are sometimes specified and can be obtained in small quantities from modelmaker's suppliers, as can brass rods and piano wire. As an alternative to buying new tin sheet, you can use scrap metal from a discarded square can, for example, of cooking oil.

Plastic and acrylic

Plastic washers are a lightweight alternative to metal washers and have the advantage that you can drill the hole to the precise size you require. They are easily made from the type of hard plastic used for supermarket milk and juice containers. Clear acrylic sheets used for windows are available from doll's house suppliers, some D-I-Y shops and plastics suppliers.

·BASIC TECHNIQUES·

While this is not intended to be a comprehensive guide to all woodworking techniques, on the following pages you will find some useful general hints on the specific woodworking and toymaking techniques used in this book. It is advisable to read this section carefully before starting the projects. Use it also as a reference while working.

MAKING AND USING TEMPLATES

Most of the projects in this book provide diagrams for you to use to create your own templates for the pieces that make up each toy. Wherever possible these are shown at full size to avoid the necessity of scaling up the diagrams.

The usual method for transferring the designs to the wood is to trace the diagram from the book, making sure that you include all the information, including positions of drill holes and position guides for later assembly.

Turn the tracing paper over and shade over the reverse side of the marks with a soft pencil.

Tape the tracing paper right side uppermost to the surface of the wood and draw over the original pencil lines using firm pressure to transfer the marks to the wood. Use a pointed instrument such as the end of a pair of compasses to mark the centres of the drill holes. Remove the tracing paper and mark any further information you may need – such as reference numbers or bit sizes – on the wood.

If you wish to make a longer lasting template that you can use again, instead of transferring the traced design directly onto the wood, transfer it onto a sheet of thin card. Cut around the edge of the design. Fix this to the wood with double-sided tape and draw around the edge in pencil. Mark hole positions through the template with a sharp point, as before.

SCALING UP

Where the plans and templates are not given full size, a scale or ratio is given. Full size (100 percent) has a ratio of 1 to 1, written as 1:1; half size (50 percent) is 1:2, two thirds (66.7 percent) is 2:3 and so on. Use the following calculations to scale up the plans:

1:2 = ÷ by 1 × by 2 or enlarge on a photocopier to 200%; **3:4** = ÷ by 3 × by 4 or enlarge to 133.3%; **2:3** = ÷ by 2 × by 3 or enlarge to 150%
To work out the enlargement percentage: (scale 2:3) 3/2 × 100 = 150%; (scale 3:4) 4/3 × 100 = 133.3%, and so on.

CUTTING SOFTWOOD

Use a tenon saw for straight cuts in softwood. For saw cuts in the direction of the grain, hold the wood in a vice or with g-clamps on a bench and follow a pencil line.

For saw cuts against the grain, mark the cut with a set square and craft knife all the way around the wood. This helps to reduce kerf – ragged edges – along the cut. Rest the wood against a bench hook while you cut.

CUTTING SLOTS IN SOFTWOOD

Mark all the way around the wood with a pencil (for a slot with the grain) or with a craft knife (for a slot against the grain), using a set square for accuracy. Use a tenon saw to make parallel cuts to the depth marked. Use a coping saw to remove the waste.

USING A FRETSAW

The hand fretsaw, used for cutting plywood shapes, is one of the most important tools for the toymaker. It can be fitted with blades of different thicknesses according to the gauge of plywood to be cut. Unless specified otherwise in the instructions, use a medium blade for all the projects in this book. It is generally used in conjunction with a cutting table, clamped to the edge of the work-bench, which supports the sheet of plywood while you work.

To cut out shapes marked from the edge of the plywood, support the work on the cutting table with the edge to be cut facing you. Saw towards the bench, following the marked line. Turn the work as necessary so that you are always cutting in the same direction.

To cut holes or shapes from inside a sheet of plywood, drill a 1.5mm (¹⁄₁₆in) hole through the marked line of the hole. Remove the blade from the fretsaw and thread it through the hole. Reconnect it and saw along the marked lines as above.

DRILLING

Throughout this book it has been assumed that the reader has a simple electric hand drill. Such a drill is perfectly suitable for all the drilling tasks required in these projects. However, it is strongly recommended for safety and accuracy that it is used in a pillar drill stand with a built-in depth gauge and vice. For small holes requiring very fine bits, you need to fit a pin chuck to your drill.

GENERAL DRILLING HINTS

Unless the instructions specify otherwise, it is advisable to drill holes in plywood before cutting out the individual pieces. For holes at right angles to the surface, set the work horizontally in the vice and drill in the normal way. If you need to drill an angled hole, mark the intended path of the hole on the side of the work and align this vertically with the bit. When accuracy of angle is particularly critical, you may need to make a jig, as described in the Rolling Rattle (page 46).

Whenever you are drilling through a piece of work, place a piece of scrap plywood underneath to protect the bit and reduce kerf.

DRILLING TO DEPTH

To drill a hole to a specific depth, you normally simply set the depth gauge on your stand to the required amount. If you do not have one, or if the drill needs to be set too far from the work, you can mark the drill bit with masking tape to indicate the depth of the hole. You can then stop drilling when that point is reached.

DRILLING TO WIDTH

In toymaking, holes are drilled for a number of purposes and it is important to be aware of the reason for the hole before you start work. The hole may be to accommodate a turning dowel or rod, it may be for a dowel that needs to be a tight fit, or it may be a screw hole (see below). Be sure to select the right width bit for the job. For holes that are designed for a loose fit, for example, for the axles of a wheeled toy, you will notice that the instructions generally specify a bit size that is somewhat larger than the diameter of the dowel or rod it needs to accommodate. For holes in which a dowel is intended to fit tightly, greater accuracy is required and you should use a bit that is precisely the same size as the dowel or rod. If in doubt choose a bit that is slightly smaller than you think may be needed. It is easier to enlarge a hole or sand down the dowel to fit than it is to compensate for a hole that has been drilled too large.

SELECTING THE RIGHT BIT

For most kinds of drilling, use standard high-speed bits. For holes above 6.5mm (¼in), flat bits give a cleaner finish. A hole created with a flat bit should be drilled from both sides. Drill one side until the pointed tip just starts to protrude. Then turn the work and, using the hole as a guide, drill from the other side. Lip and spur bits, originally designed for industrial purposes, are now widely available for the home market. They produce a clean kerf-free hole and are used in the same way as flat bits.

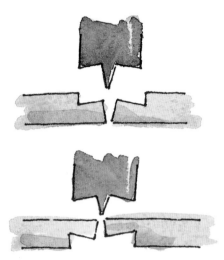

RECESSED HOLES

To drill a hole that is larger on one side than the other, first drill a hole of the larger size with a flat or lip and spur bit to the required depth. Drill the smaller second hole centred on the first hole in the usual way.

HOLE SAWS

These are used to cut extra large holes and can be used to cut out wheels without the need for a lathe. Available in a number of diameters, the hole saws fit into the chuck of a standard drill. Prepare for drilling with a hole saw by using a pair of compasses to draw the size of circle you need. Unless you need the hole to be in a specific position, make sure that the rim of the circle just touches the edge of the wood. Drill a 6.5mm (¼in) hole through the centre of the circle using a standard high-speed bit. Fit a hole saw of the required size to the drill and locate the central bit in the previously drilled hole. Drill halfway through the work and then turn and complete the drilling. Note that drilling with a hole saw creates a lot of torque, so be sure to secure your work firmly, by clamping if possible.

DRILLING SCREW HOLES

The size of bit needed for screw holes is determined by the gauge of the screw. You need to drill the hole twice. The first drilling is to the length of the screw and uses a bit that is slightly smaller than the thread. This allows the screw to "bite" into the wood. Most woodworkers learn to judge this by eye. The second drilling uses a bit that is a fraction larger than the size of the shank and is drilled to the estimated depth of the unthreaded section. Careful drilling of screw holes in this way ensures a firm fit in which the screw does not split the wood as it is inserted.

COUNTERSUNK HOLES

Some screws are designed to be countersunk, that is to lie flush to the surface of the wood. To achieve this, drill the top section of the hole a third time using a countersink bit. Judge the depth of countersink by eye, test by inserting the screw, and drill again if necessary.

CUTTING DOWELS

Mark the length of dowel required with a craft knife, and complete the cut with a junior hacksaw. Thin dowels may be cut all the way through with a craft knife.

CHAMFERING DOWELS

To ease the fit of a dowel into a hole, chamfer the end using a craft knife in the same way as you would to sharpen a pencil. Smooth the end by rolling the dowel across a block of medium glasspaper.

CHAMFERED AND BEVELLED EDGES

An accurate chamfered, or sloping, edge on softwood should be marked with a pencil line along the edge of the wood, using a protractor and adjustable set square as a guide. Holding the wood in a vice, use a block plane to remove the waste wood.

To cut mitred or bevelled corners in plywood, mark the wood as above, using a craft knife to reduce kerf. Support the wood against a bench hook and cut along the mark with a junior hacksaw.

SANDING

For a professional finish, it is important to keep your work smooth and free from kerf by sanding at regular stages. Keep four grades of glasspaper in stock for different kinds of sanding: coarse, medium, fine and extra fine. In shops you may find these numbered 50, 100, 150 and 250 respectively. Each grade is suited for a different purpose. Use coarse glasspaper for shaping and reducing size. Medium is best for removing kerf after sawing and to smooth a surface after using coarse glasspaper. Use fine

for sanding prior to painting. Extra fine glasspaper can be used as an alternative to steel wool for sanding down between coats of paint or varnish.

For ease of sanding flat surfaces and corners, make blocks of each grade of paper from scrap softwood. Round off two corners and wrap the glasspaper around the block. Secure at the back with a piece of scrap plywood, fixed with panel pins, as shown. A tri-angular sanding block made from a wedge of softwood in a similar way is useful for sanding into corners. For sanding the insides of holes, wrap glasspaper around a length of dowel.

GLUING

For all gluing work ensure clean and dust-free surfaces. Make sure that the room is well-ventilated as drying glue can give off fumes.

SOLDERING

A number of the projects have small metal parts that need to be joined by soldering. It is preferable to use a 40-watt soldering iron with general-purpose multicore solder recommended for electrical use. Clean metal surfaces to be joined with steel wool or extra fine glasspaper before soldering. Heat the joint well before applying the solder. Do not carry the solder to the joint with the iron as this evaporates the flux.

PAINTING

For painting wooden toys you need durable paints that will not harm children if the toy is handled or sucked. For the best visual impact you also need to select paints with strong, dense colours. There are a variety of paint options open to the toymaker. The paint you choose is to a large extent a matter of personal preference and availability. Throughout this book

the instructions refer only to toy-safe paints, leaving you, the reader, to decide by experimentation which materials suit you best.

Casein emulsion hobby paint. This is a water-based paint that dries to a water-resistant finish. For a more durable finish it should, however, be varnished. It has excellent covering properties and flows well for painting detail. It is a good choice for all projects where strong, flat colour is preferred. It is available from well-stocked shops.

Oil-based model enamel. Widely available from modelmaker's suppliers and D-I-Y stores, these paints provide good coverage and are highly water resistant, even when unvarnished. Use matt white enamel directly on the wood as an undercoat wherever an initial coat of white is specified. Detail may, however, be difficult to paint accurately with this type of paint.

Water-based dyes. In some cases, you may want to preserve the impression of wood. Water-based dyes, available in a variety of colours, allow the grain and character of the wood to show through. They can be applied in varying densities to produce a greater or lesser intensity of colour. These cannot, however, be used for detail.

PAINTING TIPS

Sand all surfaces with fine glasspaper before painting. Make sure that the wood is clean and free from dust before any paint or dye is applied.

Unless you are using dyes, apply an undercoat of matt enamel paint before painting in the colour of your choice. To create a paper-like surface, apply two undercoats, rubbing down with steel wool between coats.

Where more than one coat of paint is needed, always allow the first coat to dry thoroughly and rub down with steel wool or extra fine glasspaper before applying the next coat.

USING SPRUES

Small toy parts may be difficult to handle while painting. You can often get around this problem by holding the pieces on a length of spare dowel, known as a sprue, while you paint. Keep a selection of dowels of different widths approximately 100mm (4in) long for this purpose. Chamfer the ends for ease of insertion into the part to be painted. For drying the painted parts, make a softwood sprue holder through which you have drilled a number of 6.5mm (¼in) holes.

A fan heater set on low is useful for speeding up the drying process. If you place the toy, or toy part, in a cardboard box this will concentrate the warmth and cut down drying time even more. However, take care not to overheat the paint as this could cause cracking and may even warp the wood.

VARNISH

Choose polyurethane varnish, which is hard-wearing and toy-safe. It is available in matt, satin and gloss finishes and can be applied over paint or onto bare or dyed wood. For a durable finish you need two coats of varnish. If you want to achieve an exceptionally deep shine or waterproofing, you may need a third coat of gloss varnish. Apply varnish with a flat synthetic brush about 12mm (½in) wide. Do not use any brush for both paint and varnish. Allow the varnish to dry between coats, rubbing down with steel wool or extra fine glasspaper before each new application.

· UNDERWATER JIGSAW PUZZLE ·

A traditional toy for every young child, this colourful jigsaw puzzle is perfect for
encouraging hand-eye coordination and shape recognition. Because the pieces
are thick enough to stand unsupported, a child can have hours of fun
making underwater scenes from the pieces.

MATERIALS

**6.5mm (¼in) birch
plywood**
290 × 204mm
(11⅜ × 8in)

**4mm (⅛in) birch
plywood**
290 × 204mm
(11⅜ × 8in)

4mm (⅛in) dowel
140mm (5½in)

**14mm (⁹⁄₁₆in) wooden
beads with 4mm (⅛in)
hole**
(× 7)

**Toy-safe dyes or
paints**

Varnish

PVA wood glue

Double-sided tape

Masking tape

EQUIPMENT

Fretsaw

Drill and bits
4mm (⁵⁄₃₂in), 1.5mm (¹⁄₁₆in)

Glasspaper

G-clamps (optional)

Craft knife

TEMPLATES

The templates here are shown at 60 percent, or a ratio of 3:5, so scale them up as necessary.

PARTS LIST

1. **Base** 4mm ($\frac{1}{8}$in) birch plywood
2. **Puzzle frame** 6.5mm ($\frac{1}{4}$in) birch plywood
3. **Puzzle pieces** 6.5mm ($\frac{1}{4}$in) birch plywood
4. **Handle shafts** 4.5mm ($\frac{1}{8}$in) dowel
5. **Handles** Wooden beads

1 Use masking tape to sandwich together the two sheets of plywood, with the thicker sheet on top. Round off the corners with a fretsaw and sand the edges. Separate the two sheets.

2 Make paper templates of the puzzle pieces (3) and use double-sided tape to fix these to the upper surface of the 6.5mm ($\frac{1}{4}$in) plywood. Allow at least 6.5mm ($\frac{1}{4}$in) between the templates and the edge of the plywood.

3 Using the 4mm ($\frac{5}{32}$in) bit, drill the large holes in the templates through the plywood. Then drill the smaller holes marked on the templates, using the 1.5mm ($\frac{1}{16}$in) bit.

4 Using a fretsaw fitted with a fine blade, cut out the outline of each piece, following the direction indicated by the arrows on the templates. Lightly sand all pieces.

6 Paint or dye all pieces, including the background, as shown in the photographs, or in colours of your choice. Allow to dry.

5 Cut the dowel into seven 19mm (¾in) lengths. Glue a bead to one end of each piece, ensuring that the dowel extends all the way through the bead. Glue the other end of each dowel into the holes on the right side of each jigsaw shape. You may need to apply pressure in a vice to make sure that the dowel extends through the entire length of the hole so that the bead touches the surface of the piece. Wipe off any excess glue with a damp cloth.

7 Spread PVA wood glue thinly and evenly over the entire undersurface of the 6.5mm (¼in) plywood. Press the two sheets of ply together, making sure the edges are flush. Wipe away any excess glue immediately with a damp cloth. Tape or clamp the pieces together firmly until the glue is dry. Finally, apply two or three coats of varnish to all visible surfaces.

· SPACEWALKER ·

Its easy to imagine yourself taking a gentle spacewalk into the outer reaches of the galaxy with this wonderfully simple toy. Place the astronaut on one end of the frame and set him on his journey to the stars with a little tap. Now watch him roll rhythmically along the star-decorated frame until he comes to rest in the notches at the end.

EQUIPMENT

Fretsaw

Tenon saw

Coping saw

Drill and bit
6.5mm (¼in)

Glasspaper

Craft knife

MATERIALS

6.5mm (¼in) birch plywood
450 × 400mm (18 × 15in)

4mm (⅛in) birch plywood
100 × 100mm (4 × 4in)

6.5mm (¼in) dowel
100mm (4in)

18mm (¾in) softwood
450 × 50mm (18 × 2in)

PVA wood glue

Toy-safe paints

Varnish

TEMPLATES AND PLANS

These templates are shown full size, with a cutting plan included below.

6·5mm (¼") Ø

89mm
(3½")

③

①

Parts List

1. Sides (2) 6.5mm (¼in) birch plywood

2. Base 18mm (¾in) softwood

3. Astronaut 4mm (⅛in) birch plywood

4. Astronaut pivot 6.5mm (¼in) dowel

1 Make a template for the astronaut (3) and mark it on the 4mm (⅛in) birch plywood. Drill a hole with a 6.5mm (¼in) bit in the position marked and then use a fretsaw to cut out the shape.

2 Mark two pieces measuring 450 × 75mm (18 × 3in) on the 6.5mm (¼in) birch plywood for the sides (1), and stick the two sides together with double-sided tape. Make templates from the star shapes and draw these onto one of the sides. Cut out the star shapes through both layers using a coping saw.

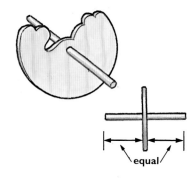

5 Round off the ends of the dowel. Smear a little glue onto the middle of the dowel and push it through the hole in the astronaut so that the ends protrude equally on each side.

3 With the two sides still taped together, secure them in a vice and cut a v-shaped notch in the top of both pieces with a tenon saw, about 12mm (½in) from one end. Plane and sand all the straight edges until they are smooth. Separate the pieces.

PAINTING THE PARTS

4 Glue the sides to the softwood base, making sure that the sides remain vertical and parallel.

6 Give all the pieces two coats of white paint. When dry, paint the sides and the base in dark blue. Do not attempt to gain a uniform finish, but rather stipple and smudge the paint to create a more varied effect. While the paint is still wet, stipple some pink into some of the paler areas and some yellow into others. When the background is dry, add some extra distant stars with dots of white.

7 Paint the astronaut in white. When this is dry add the details of the spacesuit, as illustrated, on both sides. When all parts are dry, apply two coats of varnish.

· PULL-ALONG GIRAFFE ·

Here we have a miniature version of the popular pull-along toy. This intricately painted giraffe is as much for decoration as play. Both adults and children will be charmed by the exotic bird riding on the back of its long-necked friend.
The simple wheeled construction can easily be adapted
for use with other animals of your own design.

MATERIALS

6.5mm (¼in) birch plywood
200 × 250mm (8 × 10in)

18mm (¾in) softwood
75 × 75mm (3 × 3in)

5mm (³⁄₁₆in) dowel
200mm (8in)

4mm (⅛in) dowel
50mm (2in)

6.5mm (¼in) dowel
25mm (1in)

2 screw eyes

PVA wood glue

Toy-safe paints

Varnish

EQUIPMENT

Fretsaw

Tenon saw

Drill and bits
3.5mm (⅛in), 5mm (³⁄₁₆in)

Glasspaper

Round-nosed pliers

Craft knife

TEMPLATES

All the parts here are shown full size, so you can trace them direct
from the page.

3MM (1/8) Ø

1

3MM (1/8") Ø

2

3MM (1/8") Ø

4

5MM (3/16") Ø

5

3

7MM (9/32")
Ø

1. Giraffe head and neck 6.5mm (¼in) birch plywood

2. Giraffe body 18mm (¾in) softwood

3. Giraffe leg (4) 6.5mm (¼in) birch plywood

4. Bird 6.5mm (¼in) birch plywood

5. Wheel (4) 6.5mm (¼in) birch plywood

6. Wheel axle (2) 5mm (³⁄₁₆in) dowel

7. Handle shaft 5mm (³⁄₁₆in) dowel

8. Handle cross-bar 6.5mm (¼in) dowel

9. Neck dowel 4mm (⅛in) dowel

10. Bird dowel 4mm (⅛in) dowel

11. Handle connector Screw eyes

1 Make templates for the parts and transfer these to the type of wood indicated. Drill all marked holes with the appropriate bit and use a coping saw to cut out the plywood parts. Cut two 50mm (2in) lengths of 5mm (³⁄₁₆in) dowel for the axles (6).

2 Hold the head and neck (1) against the softwood block on which you have marked the body in the corner where it will be positioned. Mark the curve on the corner of the body so that when it is cut the two parts will fit snugly. Cut out the body with a fretsaw.

3 Clamp the neck upside down in a vice and drill a hole about 10mm (³⁄₈in) deep with a 3.5mm (⅛in) bit. Glue a 19mm (¾in) length of 4mm (⅛in) dowel (9) into the hole.

4 Hold the neck against the body in the position marked previously and mark the line of the neck dowel on the body.

5 Clamp the body in a vice with the marked corner uppermost so that the line of the neck dowel is vertical. Using this line as a guide, drill a 3.5mm (⅛in) hole in the centre of body to a depth of about 10mm (³⁄₈in). Adjust the position and drill a hole in the centre of the giraffe's back to the same depth for the bird dowel (10). Apply glue to the underside of the neck and to the exposed end of the neck dowel and insert into the hole in the body.

6 Apply glue to the inner surface of the upper part of the two front legs. Position them on either side of the body and, before the glue has dried, pass one of the axles (6) through the holes. Adjust the positions of the legs, making sure that the leg holes align. Allow to dry with the axle in place. Repeat for the back legs.

7 Cut a 25mm (1in) length of 6.5mm (¼in) dowel for the handle cross-bar (8). Drill a hole through the centre with a 5mm (³⁄₁₆in) bit. Cut a 64mm (2½in) length of 5mm (³⁄₁₆in) dowel for the handle shaft (7) and glue one end of this into the cross-bar.

PAINTING AND ASSEMBLY

This is a decorative rather than robust plaything. Don't forget some feathery detail on the bird.

8 Sand all edges smooth and apply two coats of white paint to all the wooden parts. Thread the wheels onto some scrap dowel for ease of handling while painting.

9 Paint the parts as shown. Allow the background orange of the giraffe and the blue of the wheels to dry before painting the patterns. A dot of gold paint at the centre of each of the blue diamonds and in the spokes of the wheels creates a jewel-like effect. Don't forget to paint the giraffe's tail in black. When the paint is dry, apply a coat of varnish.

10 Insert the axles through the legs. Apply glue inside the holes in the wheels and fix them over the axles.

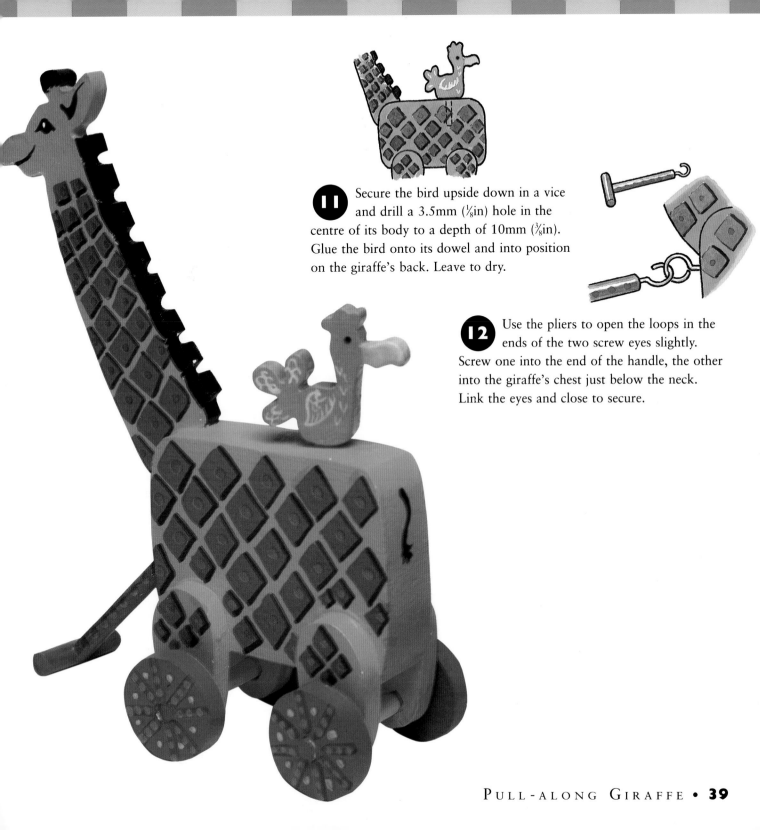

11 Secure the bird upside down in a vice and drill a 3.5mm (⅛in) hole in the centre of its body to a depth of 10mm (⅜in). Glue the bird onto its dowel and into position on the giraffe's back. Leave to dry.

12 Use the pliers to open the loops in the ends of the two screw eyes slightly. Screw one into the end of the handle, the other into the giraffe's chest just below the neck. Link the eyes and close to secure.

· WADDLING DUCKS ·

The design of this charming set of waddling farmyard ducks has its origins in Bavaria in southern Germany and examples of toys of this kind can be seen in the Nuremberg Toy Museum. The surprisingly lifelike waddling motion is produced simply by sliding the parallel handles that form the base to which the ducks are fixed.

MATERIALS

4mm (⅛in) birch plywood
250 × 100mm
(10 × 4in)

Softwood
50 × 25 × 150mm
(2 × 1 × 6in)

4mm (⅛in) birch dowel
75mm (3in)

16mm (⅝in) gimp pins brass or mild steel
(× 6)

Rapid-drying epoxy resin

Toy-safe paints

Varnish

PVA wood glue

EQUIPMENT

Tenon saw

Fretsaw

Drill and bits
1.2mm (³⁄₆₄in), 3.2mm (⅛in), 6.5mm (¼in)

Pin chuck

Needle-nosed pliers

Rasp or coarse glasspaper

Glasspaper

The scale here is 75 percent, or 3:4. Use the top elevation as a positional guide.

232mm (9⅛")

17mm (11/16")

6·5mm (¼") ∅

3·5 mm (⅛") ∅

1·2mm (³/₆₄") ∅

1·2 mm (³/₆₄") ∅

3·5 mm (⅛") ∅

6·5mm (¼") ∅

Parts List

1. **Duck body** (3) Softwood
2. **Duck head** (3) 4mm (⅛in) birch plywood
3. **Duck feet** (3) 4mm (⅛in) birch plywood
4. **Handles** (2) 4mm (⅛in) birch plywood
5. **Fixing dowels** (3) 4mm (⅛in) birch dowel
6. **Pivots** (6) 16mm (⅝in) gimp pins

1 Trace three copies of the template for the duck bodies (1) and mark out the shapes on the 50mm (2in) side of the softwood.

2 Place the wood in a vice and use a tenon saw to separate the body pieces. Do not attempt to shape them yet.

3 Now use a rasp or coarse glasspaper to shape the body profile of each piece, following the lines of the template.

4 Round the front of the body and form the tail into a point. When you are satisfied with the shape, sand the bodies smooth with fine glasspaper.

5 Drill holes in each body piece as indicated, using 6.5mm (¼in) and 3mm (⅛in) bits to a depth of 8mm (⁵⁄₁₆in). Make sure that the holes are at right angles to the horizontal by packing some scrap wood under the curves of the body as you work.

6 Trace and transfer three copies of the head template (2) to the plywood. Place the templates so as to allow for a "sprue" that links the pieces together. Cut out the shapes and sprue, using a fretsaw.

8 Paint all the parts as required, allowing each colour to dry before applying the next. Stand the pieces to dry in a rack made from scrap softwood. When you have completed the painting, apply two coats of varnish.

7 Cut out the feet (3) in the same way and drill the holes indicated with a 6.5mm (¼in) and 1.2mm (³⁄₆₄in) bit. Cut out the handles (4), allowing about 25mm (1in) extra at the end for holding during painting.

9 Cut the plywood parts from the sprue with a fretsaw and trim the handles. Touch up the paintwork, if necessary.

loose fit gimp pin

10 Position the feet on the handles as shown, and secure with gimp pins. Hammer these through the small holes in the feet and through the handles so that the ends protrude on the underside of the handles. Bend the ends over with pliers, and gently hammer them into the wood. The nails should be loose enough for the feet to move.

11 Apply glue inside the holes in the top of the body pieces. Position the heads inside the holes, making sure that they are facing forwards. Allow to dry.

12 Cut three 16mm (⅝in) lengths of dowel and insert a dowel into the hole in the centre of each of the feet. Roughen the underside of the body pieces and the area around the holes in the feet with glasspaper. Apply glue to the underside of the body pieces and position each piece over the dowels on the feet, facing forward. Allow to dry.

· ROLLING RATTLE ·

This decorative and sturdy toy uses very few pieces, and its simple construction makes it an ideal project for a novice wood-worker. Its simplicity and attractive colours will delight a young child, providing hours of amusement.

EQUIPMENT

Fretsaw

Tenon saw

Drill and bit
6.5mm (¼in)

Mouth spray diffuser

G-clamps

Glasspaper

Set square

Protractor

Cocktail stick

MATERIALS

9mm (⅜in) birch plywood
84 × 170mm
(3⁵⁄₁₆ × 6⅝in)

6.5mm (¼in) birch dowel
330mm (13in)

19mm (¾in) wooden beads with 7mm (⁹⁄₃₂in) holes
(× 4)

Thin card
90 × 90mm
(3½ × 3½in)

32mm (1¼in) scrap wood
45 × 40mm
(1¾ × 1½in)

22mm (⅞in) scrap softwood
120 × 140mm
(4¾ × 5½in)

Paint primer

Toy-safe paints

Varnish

PVA wood glue

Double-sided tape

All the templates are shown full size (1:1), except for the spiral spraying guide, which is 66.7 percent (2:3).

A

40mm
(1½")

50°

←— 45mm (1¾") —→

A

14mm
(9/16")

< 14mm >
(9/16")

32mm
(1¼")

50mm
(1¾")

80mm (3⁵/₃₂")

84mm
(3⁵/₁₆")

14mm
(9/16")

←— 19mm (¾") —→

120mm (4²³/₃₂")

75mm (2¹⁵/₁₆")

50°

9mm
(3/8")

B

70mm
(2¾")

←————— 84mm (3⁵/₁₆") —————→

1. Bases (2) Birch plywood

2. Struts (4) Birch dowel

3. Rattles (4) Wooden beads

MAKING THE PARTS

1 Apply two coats of varnish to the dowel. When dry, cut into four 78mm (3$\frac{1}{16}$in) lengths and rub the last 6.5mm ($\frac{1}{4}$in) at each end with glasspaper. Cut the plywood into two 84 × 84mm (3$\frac{5}{16}$ × 3$\frac{5}{16}$in) squares.

2 To make the drilling jig, cut the 22mm ($\frac{7}{8}$in) scrap wood in half to give pieces B and C measuring 120 × 70mm (4$\frac{3}{4}$ × 2$\frac{3}{4}$in). Using the template as a guide, cut the wedge out of piece B.

3 Drill a vertical hole with a 6.5mm ($\frac{1}{4}$in) bit through the 32mm (1$\frac{1}{4}$in) scrap wood as shown.

4 Then cut the piece in half diagonally with a tenon saw to form a wedge shape (piece A).

6 Place the drill bit through the hole in the jig (piece A) and use tape to mark the top of the bit when the clearance between its end and piece B is about 2mm ($\frac{5}{64}$in).

5 Glue pieces B and C together, then fix piece A to B and C with masking tape, as shown. Hold this firm with a small G-clamp.

7 Place one plywood square in the slot and clamp firmly in position. Drill through the hole until the bit reaches the mark. Turn the square and repeat until you have drilled a hole in each corner. Drill the second square in the same way.

8 Tape the squares together and, using template D or compasses, draw and cut out an 80mm (3⅛in) diameter circle. Separate the pieces (1) and smooth the edges.

9 Paint the rim of each disc with two coats of primer and, when dry, apply two coats of blue paint, sanding between coats. Allow to dry.

10 Cut two templates (E) from thin card. Fix these to the (undrilled) faces of the discs with thin strips of double-sided tape. Lightly spray them with diluted red paint. When dry, apply a further light coat, if needed.

11 Thread two beads onto a piece of spare dowel or rod and spray one side with red paint. Wash the diffuser. Turn the beads and spray the other side with diluted blue paint. Spray the remaining two beads blue on one side and green on the other. When the paint is dry, varnish all parts. Avoid getting varnish in the holes. Allow to dry.

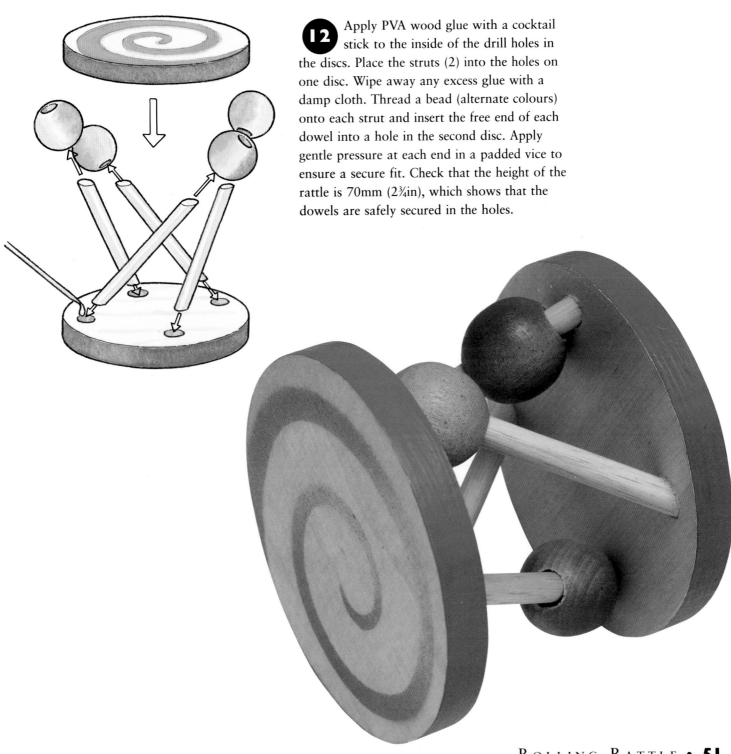

12 Apply PVA wood glue with a cocktail stick to the inside of the drill holes in the discs. Place the struts (2) into the holes on one disc. Wipe away any excess glue with a damp cloth. Thread a bead (alternate colours) onto each strut and insert the free end of each dowel into a hole in the second disc. Apply gentle pressure at each end in a padded vice to ensure a secure fit. Check that the height of the rattle is 70mm (2¾in), which shows that the dowels are safely secured in the holes.

· MONSTER ROCKET ·

This easily made toy "magically" transforms from a friendly monster to a space-age rocket. Attractively designed in bright colours, it provides lots of fun for young children, who will happily occupy themselves, pulling out the different elements to create the plaything of their choice.

TEMPLATES AND PLANS

These templates are at 50 percent, or 1:2. Use the cutting guide to minimize wastage.

ALL HOLES
4mm (5/32") Ø → O F

1·5mm (1/16") Ø

1–4. Monster/rocket side (4) 4mm (⅛in) plywood

5. Right rocket wing 4mm (⅛in) plywood

6. Left rocket wing 4mm (⅛in) plywood

7. Monster back 4mm (⅛in) plywood

8. Rocket flame/monster tail 4mm (⅛in) plywood

9. Monster feet (2) 4mm (⅛in) plywood

10. Monster head/rocket nose cone 4mm (⅛in) plywood

1 Cut the dowel to the following lengths: three 8mm ($\frac{5}{16}$in) pieces; two 12mm ($\frac{1}{2}$in) pieces; three 22mm ($\frac{7}{8}$in) pieces; two 31mm ($1\frac{3}{16}$in) pieces.

2 Trace the templates and use double-sided tape to fix them to the plywood. Use a fretsaw to cut between the shapes.

4 With piece no. 1 on top, drill hole B through all four pieces, using the same bit. Insert the other 31mm ($1\frac{3}{16}$in) length of dowel into this hole.

3 Drill hole A through the template on each body piece (1, 2, 3 and 4) using a 4mm ($\frac{5}{32}$in) bit. Sandwich all four pieces together in that order and insert a 31mm ($1\frac{3}{16}$in) length of dowel through the hole to line up the pieces. Secure with masking tape.

5 Using a fretsaw with a medium blade, cut out the body shape following the template for piece no. 1. Separate the pieces.

6 Cut out the centre of piece no. 4 by drilling a 1.5mm ($\frac{1}{16}$in) hole and feeding the fretsaw blade through.

7 Insert the dowels through holes A and B in pieces 1, 2 and 3 to ensure correct alignment. Sand the dowels to ease the fit, if necessary. Tape the pieces together and drill holes C and D through all three pieces with a 4mm ($\frac{5}{32}$in) bit. Remove piece no. 4 and replace with no. 1. Secure with tape and drill hole E. Continue drilling the holes in sequence through the different combinations of body pieces as shown. Remove templates.

8 Arrange the body pieces and insert the dowels into the holes, as shown, flush to the underside of each piece. Apply glue to the rim of the dowel ends to secure. Wipe away any excess glue with a damp cloth.

9 Drill the holes marked in pieces 5 to 10 with a 4mm (⁵⁄₃₂in) bit. If the holes in pieces 5 and 6 are not positioned precisely as on the templates, reposition the templates so that the holes marked are exactly over the drilled holes. Cut out the pieces with a fretsaw.

10 Lightly sand all pieces. Paint both sides of all pieces and any dowel ends that will show in the colours indicated. Paint a number 6, or any number of your choice, within an oval on the reverse side of piece 3. Varnish all invisible parts if required, except the stems of the dowels.

11 When dry, assemble the pieces, with washers placed between the moving parts. When you have checked that all the parts move in and out of the body freely, dismantle. Reassemble in stages as illustrated, putting a small dab of glue on the rims of the dowel ends as you work. Make sure that none of the dowels are proud of the surface.

· FLYING SWAN ·

Nothing can beat the exhilarating sight of a flock of swans in full flight. Recreate this experience in your own home with this graceful bird that rhythmically flaps its wings when hung from the ceiling. This is a superb toy for both adults and children that is not hard to make, either from the woodworking point of view, or that of the decoration.

MATERIALS

6.5mm (¼in) birch plywood
610 × 610mm (24 × 24in)

15mm (⅝in) dowel
450mm (18in)

Large wooden bead with 9mm (⅜in) hole

Brass curtain ring

String
750mm (30in)

Nylon fishing line
2.5m (10ft)

Toy-safe paints

PVA wood glue

Double-sided tape

EQUIPMENT

Fretsaw

Drill and bits
2mm (⁵⁄₆₄in), 4mm (⁵⁄₃₂in)

Glasspaper

Scissors

TEMPLATES

These templates are shown at 30 percent, or 3:10. A cutting guide is also shown.

>| |< 6.5 MM (¼")

620 MM (24")

540 MM (21¼")

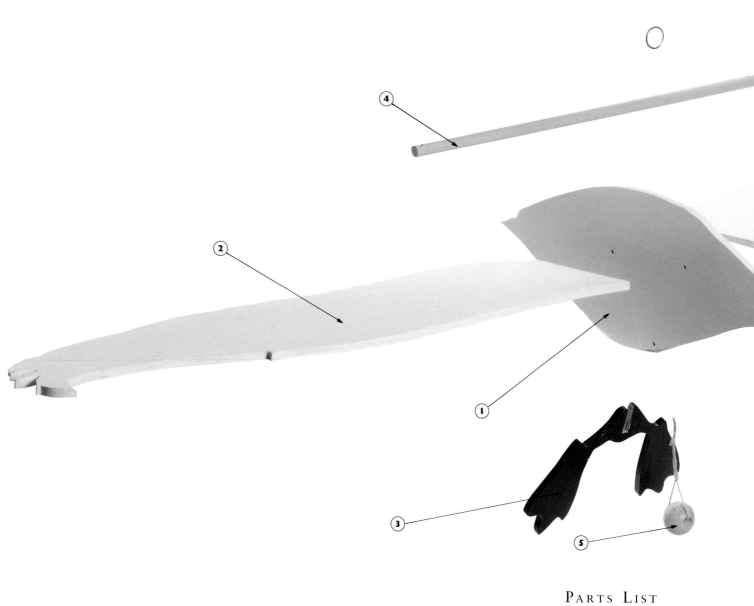

Parts List

1. **Body** 6.5mm (¼in) birch plywood
2. **Wing (2)** 6.5mm (¼in) birch plywood
3. **Feet** 6.5mm (¼in) birch plywood
4. **Dowel** 15mm (⅝in) dowel
5. **Pulling bead** Wooden bead

②

1 Make templates for the body (1), one wing (2) and feet (3) by scaling up the diagrams (see Basic techniques). Mark the body piece on the plywood and drill the holes specified with a 2mm (⁵⁄₆₄in) bit. Cut out the shape with a fretsaw.

2 Cut the remaining plywood so that you have two pieces large enough for the wing template. Fix the two pieces together with double-sided tape and mark the wing on the upper surface. Drill the specified holes through both layers with a 2mm (⁵⁄₆₄in) bit, and cut out the wing shape with a fretsaw.

3 Mark the feet on a single sheet of the remaining plywood and cut out with a fretsaw. Sand all parts to a smooth finish.

PAINTING THE PARTS

4 Apply two coats of white paint to all the plywood parts. Paint the body and wings with white top coat and paint the feet black. When the white paint is dry, add the details of the eyes and beak on both sides of the head.

ASSEMBLY

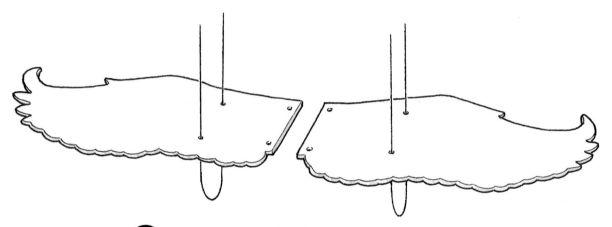

5 Cut two 1m (40in) lengths of nylon fishing line and thread them through the central holes in the wings, as shown.

6 Cut two more pieces of nylon each about 150mm (6in) long and knot them around the holes on the inner edge of one wing, leaving loose ends of approximately equal length.

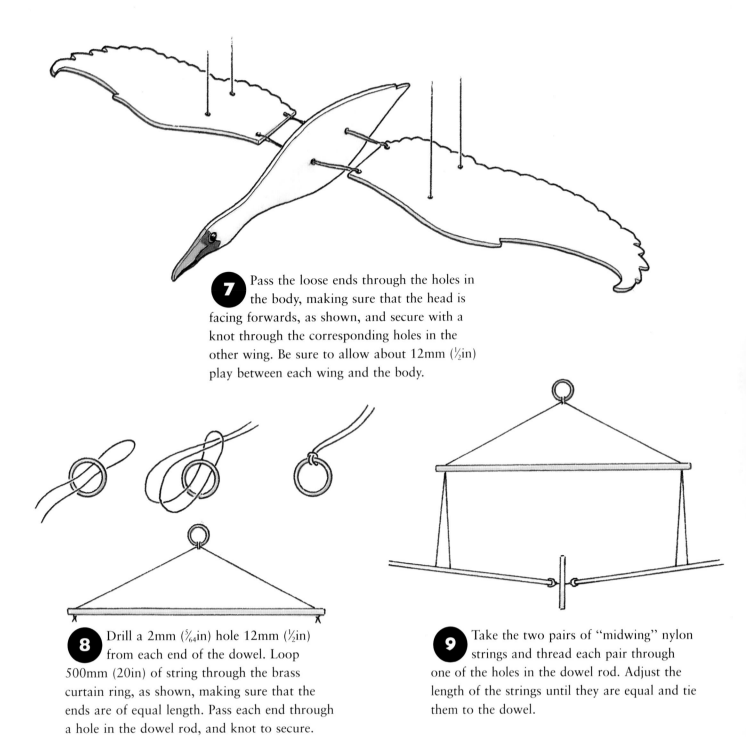

7 Pass the loose ends through the holes in the body, making sure that the head is facing forwards, as shown, and secure with a knot through the corresponding holes in the other wing. Be sure to allow about 12mm ($\frac{1}{2}$in) play between each wing and the body.

8 Drill a 2mm ($\frac{5}{64}$in) hole 12mm ($\frac{1}{2}$in) from each end of the dowel. Loop 500mm (20in) of string through the brass curtain ring, as shown, making sure that the ends are of equal length. Pass each end through a hole in the dowel rod, and knot to secure.

9 Take the two pairs of "midwing" nylon strings and thread each pair through one of the holes in the dowel rod. Adjust the length of the strings until they are equal and tie them to the dowel.

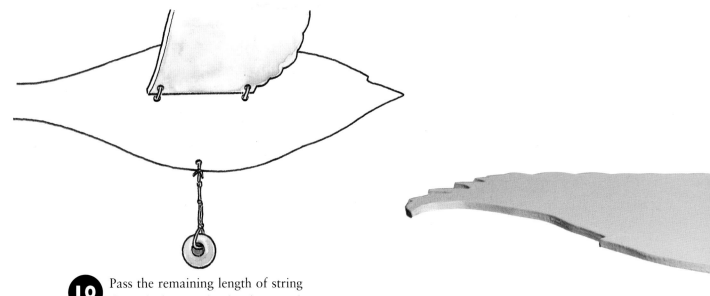

10 Pass the remaining length of string through the wooden bead. Knot the two ends together several times as shown and secure to the hole in the underside of the body.

11 Slot the feet onto the body in the position indicated on the template. Glue to secure, if necessary. Suspend the whole assembly from the curtain ring, secured perhaps to a hook in the ceiling. Gently pull and release the bead to set the wings flapping.

· ROOSTER ROLLER ·

As you roll the wheels of this colourful comic rooster, the wings flap alternately and the clicking of the cams makes a soft clucking noise. Very simple to make, this toy will delight any young child.

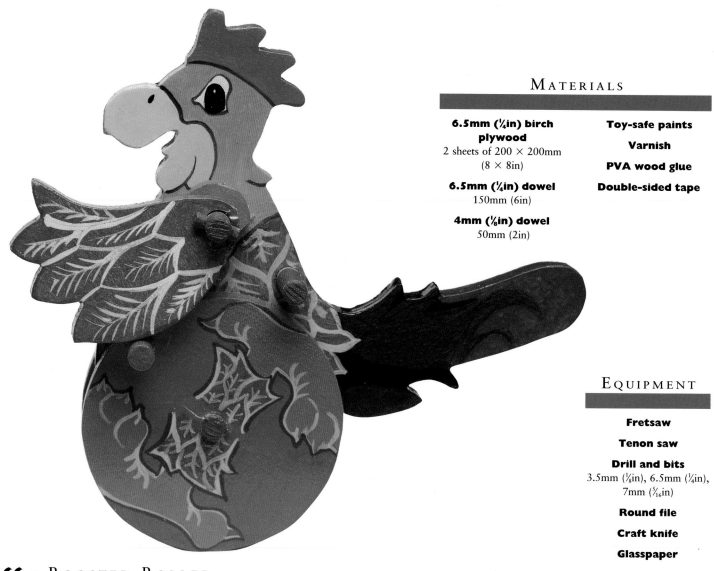

MATERIALS

6.5mm (¼in) birch plywood
2 sheets of 200 × 200mm
(8 × 8in)

6.5mm (¼in) dowel
150mm (6in)

4mm (⅛in) dowel
50mm (2in)

Toy-safe paints

Varnish

PVA wood glue

Double-sided tape

EQUIPMENT

Fretsaw

Tenon saw

Drill and bits
3.5mm (⅛in), 6.5mm (¼in),
7mm (⁵⁄₁₆in)

Round file

Craft knife

Glasspaper

TEMPLATES

All parts here are full size, so you can trace them straight from the page.

|<17mm (¹¹⁄₁₆")>| |<17mm (¹¹⁄₁₆")>|

6mm
-(¼")-
Ø
3mm(⅛")

④

7mm (⁹⁄₆₄") Ø

6mm (¼") Ø

6mm (¼")
Ø

①

②

7mm (⁹⁄₆₄")
Ø

6mm (¼")
Ø

66mm
(2⅝")

←6mm (¼") Ø

←6mm (¼") Ø

←6mm (¼") Ø

←6mm (¼") Ø

③

1. Rooster body 6.5mm (¼in) birch plywood

2. Wing (2) 6.5mm (¼in) birch plywood

3. Wheel (2) 6.5mm (¼in) birch plywood

4. Spacer (2) 6.5mm (¼in) birch plywood

5. Shoulder shaft 6.5mm (¼in) dowel

6. Wing stop 6.5mm (¼in) dowel

7. Wheel axle 6.5mm (¼in) dowel

8. Cam (2) 6.5mm (¼in) dowel

9. Wing retainer (2) 4mm (⅛in) dowel

1 Make templates of the parts from the diagrams. Fix the two sheets of 6.5mm (¼in) birch plywood together with double-sided tape. Transfer the designs onto the plywood.

2 Drill all marked holes with the size of bit specified, and cut out the shapes with a fretsaw. Separate the two layers of plywood and sand the parts smooth with fine glasspaper. Discard the spare rooster body (1) or use as scrap.

3 Measure and cut the 6.5mm (¼in) dowel into the following lengths: 45mm (1¾in) (wing stop – 6); 70mm (2¾in) (shoulder shaft – 5); 25mm (1in) (wheel axle – 7); 2 × 18mm (¾in) (cams – 8). Cut the 4mm (⅛in) dowel into two lengths of 12mm (½in) for the wing retainers (9). Smooth the ends of each dowel with fine glasspaper.

4 Drill a 3.5mm (⅛in) hole through the shoulder shaft dowel (5), 5mm (³⁄₁₆in) from each end.

5 Apply two coats of white paint to all parts and allow to dry. Following the illustrations, lightly draw in the details of the painted decoration, using a pencil. Paint the parts in the colours shown, using a fine synthetic brush for the details.

6 Paint the head as follows: yellow beak; red comb; white outer eye; black inner eye; orange head and neck. When dry, outline in dark brown.

7 Stipple light brown on the body to give a feathery effect by dabbing the wet paint with a brush. When dry, paint feathers in yellow. Use light and dark green with curved strokes to suggest long tail feathers.

8 The wheels are bright red with legs and feet overpainted in yellow. Be sure to paint the feet as shown so that the rooster will appear to "walk" when the wheels turn.

9 Paint the inside surfaces of the wings the same brown as the body. For the outside surfaces, mix a little red with the brown. Stipple this in the same way as for the body. When dry, use white paint for the feather pattern, as shown.

10 Paint the handle (tip of tail) dark brown. When dry, apply two coats of varnish to all parts, except dowels.

11 Apply glue inside the outer holes in each wheel and insert the cams (8). Apply glue inside the upper holes in the body and insert the wing stop (6) and shoulder shaft (5), ensuring that the ends of each dowel protrude equally on each side.

12 Slide the spacers (4) over each end of the shoulder shaft. They should be a tight fit and lie against the body, with the rounded sides uppermost.

13 Position the wings over the spacers so that they swing freely on the shaft. Ease the holes with a round file if necessary. Apply a little glue inside the holes in the ends of the shaft and insert the wing retainers (9).

14 Insert the wheel axle into the lower hole in the body and check that it moves freely. Glue the wheel axle into the central hole in one of the wheels on the opposite side from the cam. With the axle in position, glue the other wheel onto the free end so that the cams are at 180° to each other. Paint visible areas of the dowels.

· WIGGLING WATER MONSTER ·

In contrast to the terrifying creatures from the deep who, according to the ancient sea myths, attacked sailors and their boats, this spectacular water monster, with its friendly expression and lively colours, is a most unfrightening play companion. Mount the base on the wall and simply push the dowel rod to see this cheerful creature wiggle its way through the waves.

EQUIPMENT

Fretsaw

Tenon saw

Drill and bits
6.5mm (¼in), 7mm (⁵⁄₁₆in)

Round-nosed pliers

Glasspaper

Round file (optional)

MATERIALS

6.5mm (¼in) birch plywood
750 × 150mm (30 × 6in)

6.5mm (¼in) birch dowel
610mm (24in)

Brass screw eyes (× 2)

18mm (¾in) birch balls (× 6)

Toy-safe paints

PVA wood glue

Varnish

TEMPLATES

Parts 1 to 4 are shown at 50 percent, or 1:2, part 5 is at
30 percent, or 3:10.

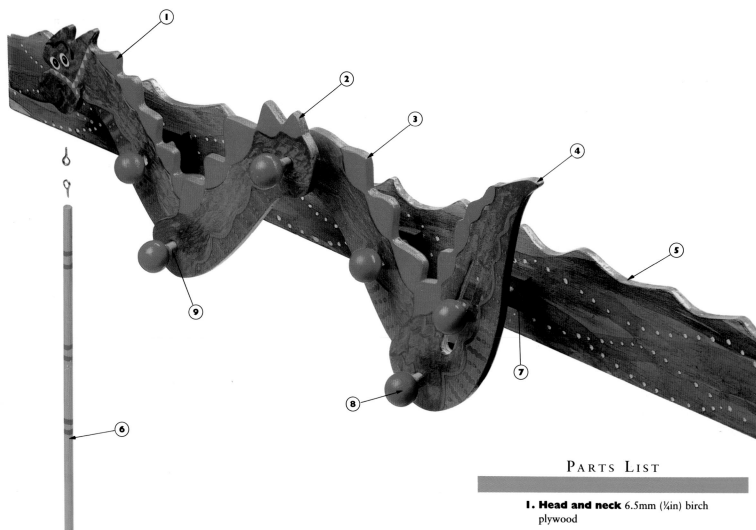

1. Head and neck 6.5mm (¼in) birch plywood

2. First body segment 6.5mm (¼in) birch plywood

3. Second body segment 6.5mm (¼in) birch plywood

4. Tail 6.5mm (¼in) birch plywood

5. Base 6.5mm (¼in) birch plywood

6. Push rod 6.5mm (¼in) birch dowel

7. Spacers (3) 6.5mm (¼in) birch plywood

8. Retainers (6) 18mm (¾in) birch balls

9. Pegs (6) 6.5mm (¼in) birch dowel

MAKING THE PARTS

1 Make templates from the diagrams and transfer the shapes onto the 6.5mm (¼in) birch plywood. Mark and drill the holes with a 7mm (⁵⁄₁₆in) or 6.5mm (¼in) bit, as specified. Cut out the slot in the tail (see Basic Techniques). Cut out all the pieces with a fretsaw and sand to a smooth finish.

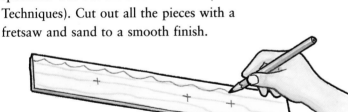

2 Mark the wave pattern along the top edge of a 75 × 610mm (3 × 24in) piece of 6.5mm (¼in) birch plywood, as shown. Drill the holes with a 6.5mm (¼in) bit and cut out the wave pattern with a fretsaw.

3 Mark out three 18mm (¾in) squares on a piece of 6.5mm (¼in) birch plywood for the spacers (7) and drill a 7mm (⁵⁄₁₆in) hole through the centre of each. Cut out the squares with a tenon saw.

4 Cut a 285mm (11in) length of 6.5mm (¼in) birch dowel for the push rod (6). Cut six 32mm (1¼in) lengths of 6.5mm (¼in) birch dowel for the pegs (9). Sand smooth.

5 Mark the centre of each ball. There is usually a slightly flattened area which is easiest to work on. Secure each ball in turn in a vice and drill a hole with a 6.5mm (¼in) bit to a depth of approximately 12mm (½in).

6 Check the fit of all pieces. The short pegs should fit tightly into the holes in the base, the spacers and the balls, but should move freely in the holes and the slot in the monster parts. If necessary, ease the holes with a round file.

PAINTING THE PIECES

Make your monster as bright and cheerful as you can, not forgetting a happy smiling face.

7 Apply two coats of white paint to all pieces and leave to dry. Lightly draw the features and body markings of the monster on the upper surface of the head, body and tail pieces (1–4), copying the photographs.

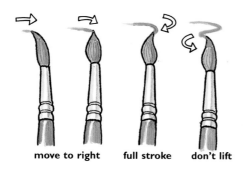

move to right   full stroke   don't lift

8 Thin some green pearlized paint with water and apply to all parts of the monster, except those areas reserved for decoration. Before the paint is dry, wiggle a medium synthetic brush in a rhythmic pattern across the painted surface to create an impression of scales. When the green paint is dry, paint the rest of the markings on the monster, as shown.

10 Glue three pegs into the holes in the base so that they are flush with the underside. Glue a spacer firmly to the base over each of the pegs.

11 With the pieces on a flat surface, glue pegs into the lower hole of the head and neck (1) and into the two outer holes of the second body segment (3) so that they are flush to the underside.

9 Paint the base in shades of diluted blues and greens to suggest waves. Don't cover the whole surface with each colour, but leave different areas unpainted with each colour to allow different mixes to show through. Allow to dry between coats. When dry, apply white dots of "surf" in wave shapes. Decorate the push rod with bands of red. When all paint is dry, varnish all painted surfaces.

12 Place the free hole in the head and neck over the left-hand peg in the base and the free hole in the second body segment over the middle hole in the base.

14 Apply glue inside the holes in the balls and secure over the free end of each peg, making sure that all parts move freely.

13 Position the first body segment (2) over the lower peg in the head and neck and the upper peg in the second body piece, as shown. Place the tail (4) over the lower peg in the second body segment with the slot over the right-hand peg in the base.

15 Screw one of the screw eyes under the monster's chin. Use pliers to open the loop of the other screw eye, and screw it into one end of the push rod. Link the screw eyes together and close the loops with pliers. Drill holes in the base, as required, to secure the assembly to a wall.

· PECKING HEN ·

This is a simplified version of a toy that is familiar to many of us. The more complicated designs have perhaps five or six birds pecking in turn, and the movement is produced by a swinging wooden ball that raises and lowers the hens' heads. In woodworking terms, this is a very easy project, whose appeal is enhanced by the decoration.

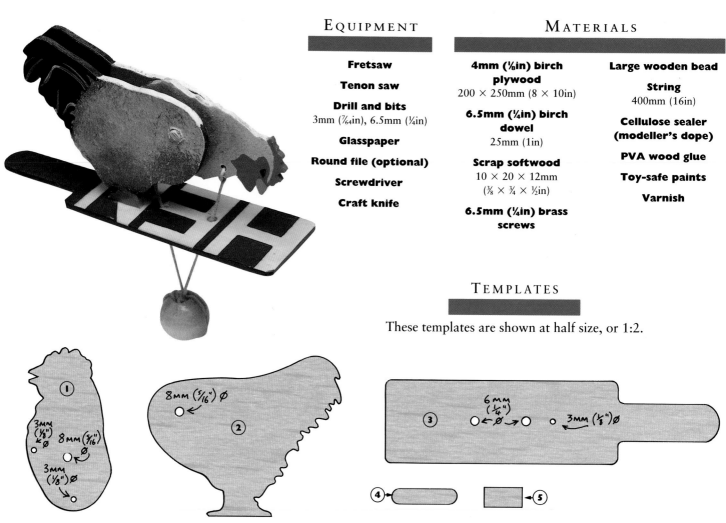

EQUIPMENT

Fretsaw

Tenon saw

Drill and bits
3mm (⁷⁄₆₄in), 6.5mm (¼in)

Glasspaper

Round file (optional)

Screwdriver

Craft knife

MATERIALS

4mm (⅛in) birch plywood
200 × 250mm (8 × 10in)

6.5mm (¼in) birch dowel
25mm (1in)

Scrap softwood
10 × 20 × 12mm
(⅜ × ¾ × ½in)

6.5mm (¼in) brass screws

Large wooden bead

String
400mm (16in)

Cellulose sealer (modeller's dope)

PVA wood glue

Toy-safe paints

Varnish

TEMPLATES

These templates are shown at half size, or 1:2.

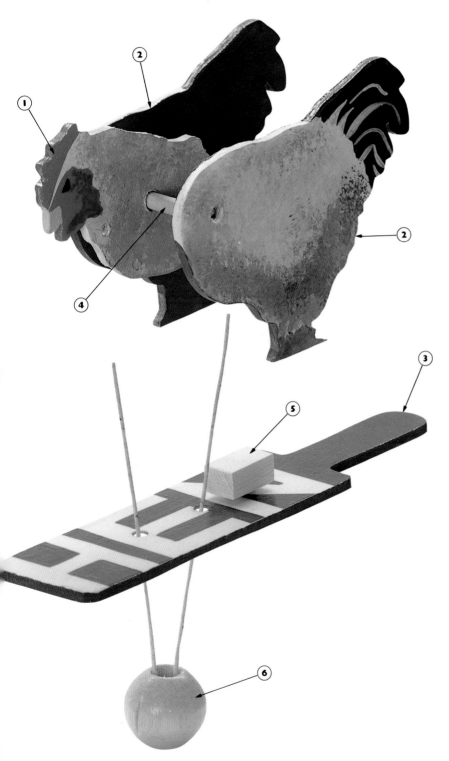

1. **Head and neck** 4mm (⅛in) birch plywood
2. **Body (2)** 4mm (⅛in) birch plywood
3. **Base** 4mm (⅛in) birch plywood
4. **Neck pivot** 6.5mm (¼in) dowel
5. **Spacer** Scrap softwood
6. **Pendulum** Wooden bead

Making the Parts

1 Make templates for the parts and transfer onto the plywood. You will need two body pieces. Drill all the holes with the size of bit specified and cut out the pieces with a fretsaw. Sand the pieces smooth.

2 Sand the piece of dowel (4) and test its fit in the large hole in the neck (1) and in the body pieces (2). The fit should be tight in the body holes but loose enough to allow free movement in the neck. If necessary, ease the holes with a round file. Apply a coat of cellulose sealer to all parts and sand lightly.

PAINTING

3 Copying from the photographs, lightly draw the details of the decoration in pencil on both sides of the head and neck, on the outer side of each of the body pieces, and on the top surface of the base.

4 Use a stiff brush to stipple white paint on the out sides of the body pieces. The covering should not be complete. Allow to dry.

5 Mix some pale blue paint and apply this with an almost dry brush over the white paint. When this is dry, apply some darker blue paint in the same way but even more sparingly. The overall effect should be lightly speckled.

6 Paint the tail black. When this is dry, apply blue and white paint in long brushstrokes to represent tail feathers. Use orange for the legs and feet and plain blue for the insides of the body pieces and the spacer.

7 Paint both sides of the neck in a similar fashion to the body. Use red for the comb and wattle, and yellow for the beak. The eye is a small black triangle. Paint the base in colours of your choice.

ASSEMBLY

8 Glue the neck dowel into the hole in one of the body pieces so that one end is flush with the outer surface.

9 Glue the spacer onto the inside of the body piece so that the short side aligns with the base of the feet.

10 Slide the neck piece onto the dowel. Glue the second body piece onto the dowel and spacer, making sure it aligns properly with the first body piece. Allow to dry.

11 Glue the hen to the base in the position shown, with the tail at the handle end of the base. Allow to dry. Drill a 6.5mm (¼in) hole through the base and into the spacer and insert a screw to strengthen the assembly.

12 Secure the bead in a vice and use a tenon saw to make two grooves on opposite sides of the bead. Cut the string into two equal lengths. Secure one to each of the small holes in the neck. Pass the ends through the holes in the base. Tie the free ends through the wooden bead as shown.

13 Touch up paintwork on dowel ends and elsewhere as necessary. Apply two coats of varnish to all external painted surfaces.

· BOAT ON THE OCEAN ·

This toy is just the thing for sailors of all ages who don't want to get their feet wet! As you turn the handle, the brightly painted ocean liner bobs its way through the rolling waves. The movement of the water is produced by the action of cams on a shaft. Vivid primary colours and strong shapes contribute to the bold impact of this toy.

MATERIALS

4mm (⅛in) birch plywood
20 × 40mm (¾ × 1½in)

Softwood
130 × 20 × 650mm
(5 × ¾ × 25in)

9mm (⅜in) dowel
510mm (20in)

5mm (³⁄₁₆in) dowel
30mm (1¼in)

4mm (⅛in) dowel
120mm (4¾in)

PVA wood glue

Masking tape

Toy-safe paints

Varnish

EQUIPMENT

Fretsaw

Tenon saw

Glasspaper

Drill and bits
4mm (⅛in), 5mm (³⁄₁₆in),
9mm (⅜in) flat bit

Round file (optional)

Pair of compasses

TEMPLATES AND PLANS

These templates are shown half size, or 1:2. Use the elevation as a guide to shaping the boat.

PARTS LIST

1. **Waves type 1 (2)** Softwood
2. **Waves type 2 (2)** Softwood
3. **Boat and wave** Softwood
4. **Sides (2)** Softwood
5. **Stand (2)** Softwood
6. **Funnel** 9mm (⅜in) dowel

7. **Cam shaft** 9mm (⅜in) dowel
8. **Axle rod** 9mm (⅜in) dowel
9. **Cams (5)** 4mm (⅛in) dowel
10. **Handle** 5mm (³⁄₁₆in) dowel
11. **Handle shaft** 4mm (⅛in) dowel
12. **Spacers (2)** 4mm (⅛in) birch plywood

MAKING THE PARTS

1 Cut the softwood with a tenon saw as shown. Mark a wavy line through the centre of each part A. Mark and drill two 9mm (³⁄₈in) holes at one end of each of these parts, as shown. Cut along the undulating line to make four wave sections (1 and 2). Sand smooth.

3 Tape the boat back into its original position on its wave and drill through the boat and partway through the wave with a 9mm (³⁄₈in) bit. Separate the parts.

4 Securing the boat in a vice, plane it to the shape shown, and sand smooth.

2 Mark out the central wave and boat (3) on the softwood. Cut along the line of the wave and drill a 9mm (³⁄₈in) hole in one end to align with the holes in the other wave pieces. Cut out the boat.

5 Cut a 180mm (7in) length of 9mm (³⁄₈in) dowel for the cam shaft (7). Drill five holes in a spiral around the shaft to a depth of 5mm (³⁄₁₆in). The easiest way to judge the positions of the holes is to drill the first hole, measure the distance to the next hole 24mm (just under 1in), and then turn the dowel until the first hole is only just visible. Mark and drill the second hole at this point. Mark and drill the other holes in the same way.

6 Cut six 14mm (⁵⁄₈in) lengths of 4mm (⅛in) dowel. Glue five of these into the holes in the middle of the shaft, leaving the end holes free. These cams should protrude by about 9mm (³⁄₈in).

8 Cut a 125mm (4⁷⁄₈in) length of 9mm (³⁄₈in) dowel for the axle rod (8). Draw two 20mm (³⁄₄in) diameter circles for the spacers (12) on the plywood. Drill a 9mm (³⁄₈in) hole through the centre of each, and cut out using a fretsaw. Arrange the wave pieces along the rod, alternating wave types and with the boat wave in the middle and the spacers on either side, as shown. Make sure that the waves move freely around the axle.

7 Drill a 9mm (³⁄₈in) hole with a flat bit through the centre of each side piece (4) and to a depth of about 14mm (⁵⁄₈in) in one (inside) corner of each piece, as shown. Insert the ends of the cog shaft (7) through the central holes of the two side pieces so that the recessed holes are opposite each other, facing inwards. Check that the shaft moves freely. Ease the holes with a round file if necessary.

9 Cut two stand pieces (5) from the softwood. Use a tenon saw to cut the basic rectangle and a fretsaw to cut the angled undersides. Cut the slots in the top of each piece (see Basic Techniques).

10 Position the axle rod and wave assembly between the side pieces, with the ends of the axle located in the recessed holes in the sides. Place the assembly onto the stand with the sides resting in the slots.

11 Turn the cam shaft to test the movement of the waves; each wave section should rise up in turn. You may need to adjust the positions of the wave pieces and cam shaft to find the optimum position. When everything is working well, make a pencil mark on the outer ends of the shaft where they emerge from the sides.

12 Dismantle the assembly. Drill a 4mm (⅛in) hole through the cam shaft close to one of the marks. Insert the remaining 14mm (⅝in) length of 4mm (⅛in) dowel as a retainer. Drill another hole for the handle at the other end of the shaft about 4mm (⅛in) from the mark towards the end.

13 Make the handle from a 30mm (1¼in) length of 5mm (³⁄₁₆in) dowel through which you have drilled a 4mm (⅛in) hole. Glue the shaft made from a 19mm (¾in) length of 4mm (⅛in) dowel into the handle.

14 Make the funnel, which also holds the boat in position, from a 64mm (2½in) length of 9mm (⅜in) dowel. This should fit snugly through the hole in the boat and into the hole in the central wave. Glue into the boat as shown, leaving the lower end protruding.

15 When you are happy with the assembly, dismantle any unglued parts. Apply two coats of white to all parts that will be visible.

16 Use different shades of blue on the waves to give a realistic sea effect. Add dots of white to the tops of some of the waves to represent surf. Leave to dry, then varnish all external surfaces. As the boat is the focal point of the toy, make it as colourful and detailed as possible.

17 When dry, reassemble the parts. Glue the protruding lower end of the funnel into the hole in the central wave. Glue the sides into the slots in the stand. Finally, glue the handle into the cam shaft, and the retaining dowel into the other end of the shaft.

· TWIZZLE ·

The movement of this colourful toy is produced by the turning force of twisted elastic bands in conjunction with the centrifugal action of two beads on threads. Simply turn the wire handle at the base of the toy to prime the mechanism, stand it upright and watch the fish turn, pause and turn again. Uncomplicated to make, this toy will amuse adults and children alike. Like many toys with moving parts, it is best to make and assemble the parts to check the mechanism before painting and carrying out the final assembly.

MATERIALS

4mm (⅛in) birch plywood
250 × 128mm
(10 × 5in)

12 × 12mm (½ × ½in) softwood
750mm (30in)

2.5mm (³⁄₃₂in) brass rod
250mm (10in)

1mm (¹⁄₃₂in) welding wire
300mm (12in)

8mm (⁵⁄₁₆in) birch dowel
200mm (8in)

Elastic bands
(× 2)
75 × 1.5mm (3 × ¹⁄₁₆in)

Cartridge paper
125 × 100mm (5 × 4in)

Scrap hard plastic

Wooden beads
5mm (³⁄₁₆in), 15mm (⅝in)

Button thread

Matchsticks

Toy-safe paints

PVA wood glue

Varnish

EQUIPMENT

Fretsaw

Tenon saw

Drill and bits
1.2mm (³⁄₆₄in),
1.5mm (¹⁄₁₆in),
2.5mm (³⁄₃₂in),
(flat) 9mm (³⁄₈in)

Pin chuck

Round-nosed pliers

Diagonal cutters

Craft knife

The templates and the plan of the winding mechanism are shown at
80 percent (4:5).

Parts List

1. **Fish** 4mm (⅛in) birch plywood
2. **Frame top** 12mm (½in) softwood
3. **Frame base** 12mm (½in) softwood
4. **Frame feet** (2) 12mm (½in) softwood
5. **Pillar** (2) 2.5mm (³⁄₃₂in) brass rod
6. **Winding handle** 1mm (¹⁄₃₂) welding wire
7. **Winding handle bearing** 8mm (⁵⁄₁₆in) birch dowel
8. **Elastic bands** (2)
9. **Elastic-band tube** Cartridge paper
10. **Band hook** 1mm (¹⁄₃₂in) welding wire
11. **Swivel shaft** 1mm (¹⁄₃₂in) welding wire
12. **Fish swivel washers** (2) Hard plastic
13. **Fish swivel shaft bead**
14. **Thread**
15. **Thread retainers** (2) Matchsticks
16. **Weights** (2) Wooden beads

1 Apply two coats of white paint to both sides of the birch plywood, sanding between coats. Allow to dry. Cut out the fish (1) from the plywood with a fretsaw, using the template as a guide. Drill the marked holes using a 1.5mm ($\frac{1}{16}$in) bit. Sand edges.

4 Locate the frame base in the notches of the feet sections so that the centre point of each foot is 25mm (1in) from the end of the frame base. Drill through the base and partway through the feet – a total depth of about 19mm ($\frac{3}{4}$in) – using a 2.5mm ($\frac{3}{32}$in) bit.

2 Cut two 90mm ($3\frac{1}{2}$in) lengths from the softwood for the feet of the frame (4). In each piece, cut a notch the same width as the wood to a depth of 4mm ($\frac{3}{16}$in).

3 Cut two 250mm (10in) lengths of softwood for the frame top and base (2 and 3). Drill a hole through the centre of the frame top using a 2.5mm ($\frac{3}{32}$in) bit. Measure 105mm ($4\frac{1}{8}$in) from the centre on both sides of the centre and drill to a depth of 9mm ($\frac{3}{8}$in). Drill a 9mm ($\frac{3}{8}$in) hole through the centre of the frame base.

5 Chisel a v-shaped groove 30mm ($1\frac{3}{16}$in) long on each side of the centre hole in the underside of the frame base, to a depth of about 3mm ($\frac{1}{8}$in).

6 Cut the wire into the following lengths: 57mm (2¼in) (swivel shaft – 11); 50mm (2in) (elastic-band hook – 10); 75mm (3in) (winding handle – 6). Use round-nose pliers to make loops in both ends of the elastic-band hook and in one end of the swivel shaft and the winding handle.

glue

7 To make the winding handle bearing (7), take the 8mm (⁵⁄₁₆in) birch dowel and chamfer one end with a craft knife. Measure 19mm (¾in) from the chamfered end and cut. Drill a 1.2mm (³⁄₆₄in) hole through the centre of this piece, and sand to finish.

9 Take a piece of 8mm (⁵⁄₁₆in) dowel and firmly roll the long edge of the cartridge paper around it once. Spread PVA glue thinned with water over the rest of the paper and continue to roll it firmly around the dowel. Allow to dry, remove dowel and trim the tube to a final length of 120mm (4¾in).

8 Make two plastic washers, about 4mm (⅛in) in diameter, from scrap hard plastic. Drill a hole in the centre of each using a 1.2mm (³⁄₆₄in) bit.

10 Spread a thin layer of wood glue inside the notch on the feet of the frame. Insert the pillars (5) through the frame base into the feet and press into position. Locate the frame top on the pillars.

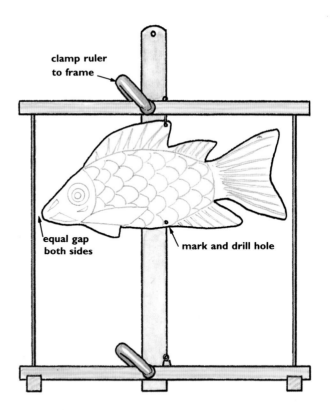

clamp ruler
to frame

equal gap
both sides

mark and drill hole

11 Use pliers to open one of the loops on the wire swivel shaft, and insert it through the middle hole in the dorsal fin of the fish. Close the loop. Insert the shaft up through the hole in the frame top. Thread the washers over the wire and then the 5mm ($\frac{3}{16}$in) wooden bead. Loop the end of the wire to secure the assembly and make sure the fish rotates smoothly.

12 Thread the winding handle through the hole in the winding handle bearing so that the existing loop is at the chamfered end. Bend the handle into a right angle as shown and insert through the hole in the frame base so that the handle fits in the groove below.

13 Stand the frame upright, with the fish hanging freely from the top. Mark the position of the lower hole in the fish at a point where it aligns vertically with the top hole and the hole in the centre of the frame base. Use a ruler to line up these points. Remember to allow approximately 4mm ($\frac{1}{8}$in) between the hole and the edge of the fish. The distance between the front of the fish and the pillar and the tail and the other pillar should be equal. Drill the hole with a 1.5mm ($\frac{1}{16}$in) bit.

turn

14 Open one loop of the elastic-band hook and insert it through the lower hole in the fish. Close around the hole. Hook two elastic bands onto the other hook and also onto the hook on the winding handle. Lay the assembly down as shown, pull out the handle and wind for about 20 turns. Stand the assembly upright and make sure the fish rotates freely between the pillars.

16 Wind handle; this time try 60 turns to allow approximately 10 minutes of movement. If the fish hits the pillars, it may not be balanced properly. If the fish does not swivel easily, check the mobility of the top bearing.

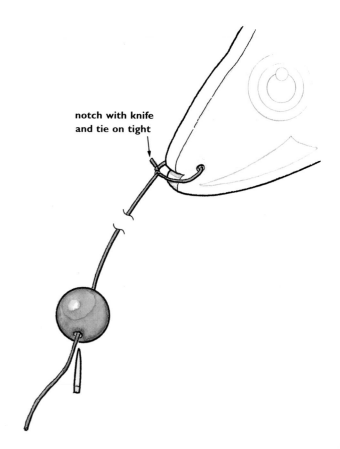

notch with knife and tie on tight

15 Tie a 200mm (8in) length of strong (button) thread into each of the holes in the head and tail of the fish, securing with a notch on the edge of the head and tail. Thread on the 15mm (⅝in) beads and secure temporarily with a sharpened matchstick about 100mm (4in) along the thread. Trim any excess thread, leaving a little spare under the beads to allow for adjustment.

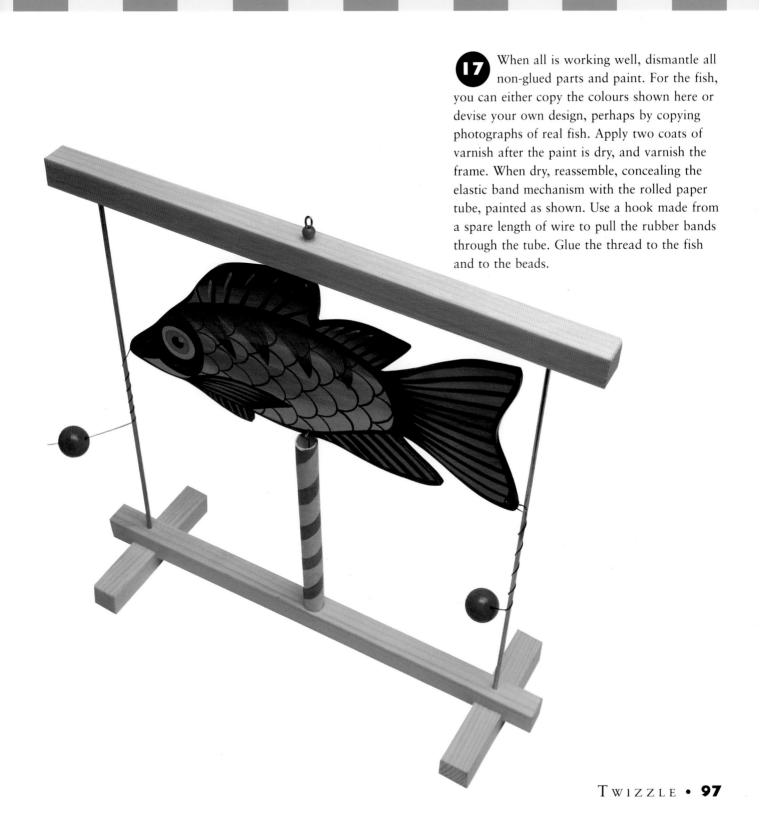

17 When all is working well, dismantle all non-glued parts and paint. For the fish, you can either copy the colours shown here or devise your own design, perhaps by copying photographs of real fish. Apply two coats of varnish after the paint is dry, and varnish the frame. When dry, reassemble, concealing the elastic band mechanism with the rolled paper tube, painted as shown. Use a hook made from a spare length of wire to pull the rubber bands through the tube. Glue the thread to the fish and to the beads.

· JUNGLE RACE ·

Based on the intriguing notion that exotic animals like to meet in jungle clearings to hold races, this effective toy is a reworking of the racing games of the 1930s. Just hook the base over the edge of a large table with the animals lined up at the other end. Wind the handle and see which creature reaches the banana-tree winning post first. The element of chance is created by the random way in which the string winds around the shaft. Never mind that this motley band of animals forms a most unlikely gathering, this fantasy game will appeal to the whole family.

9mm (⅜in) birch plywood
230 × 230mm
(9 × 9in)

4mm (⅛in) birch plywood
430 × 300mm
(17 × 12in)

8mm (⁵⁄₁₆in) birch dowel
280mm (11in)

6.5 × 6.5mm (¼ × ¼in) ramin
152mm (6in)

Thin braided nylon cord (size 2A)
8m (9yds)

25mm (1in) countersunk screws
(× 2)

12mm (½in) countersunk screws
(× 4)

12mm (½in) panel pins

Cocktail sticks
(× 10)

PVA glue

Toy-safe paints

Varnish

EQUIPMENT

Fretsaw

Tenon saw

Drill and bits
1.2mm (³⁄₆₄in), 2mm (⁵⁄₆₄in), 2.5mm (³⁄₃₂in), 4mm (⁵⁄₃₂in), 8mm (⁵⁄₁₆in), 9mm (⅜in) flat bit

Pin chuck

Screwdriver

Round file

Glasspaper

Craft knife

Set square

Tape measure or long rule

Pair of compasses

Templates and Plans

The parts on this page are at 66.7 percent, or 2:3. Those on the next page are full size.

PARTS LIST

1. **Cheetah** 4mm (⅛in) birch plywood
2. **Wallaby** 4mm (⅛in) birch plywood
3. **Ostrich** 4mm (⅛in) birch plywood
4. **Springbok** 4mm (⅛in) birch plywood
5. **Zebra** 4mm (⅛in) birch plywood
6. **Animal base** (5) 4mm (⅛in) birch plywood
7. **Animal support** (10) 6.5mm (¼in) ramin

8. **Strings** (5) Nylon cord
9. **String guide** 9mm (⅜in) birch plywood
10. **Sides** (2) 9mm (⅜in) birch plywood
11. **Base** 4mm (⅛in) birch plywood
12. **Table stop** 9mm (⅜in) birch plywood
13. **Handle** 8mm (⁵⁄₁₆in) birch dowel
14. **Handle collar** (2) 9mm (⅜in) birch plywood
15. **Banana tree** 4mm (⅛in) birch plywood
16. **Retainers** Cocktail sticks

1 Make templates for all the parts from the diagrams provided, scaling up the sizes where necessary. Cut out the parts and drill any marked holes. Countersink the marked holes in the sides (10), making sure that you drill from the outer side of each piece. Sand all edges.

2 Cut the slots in the string guide (9) using a craft knife and tenon saw (see Basic Techniques). Sand the inside edges of the slots smooth so that the cord for the strings slides easily but not too loosely inside.

3 Screw the sides to the string guide with two 25mm (1in) countersunk screws. Secure the table stop (12) to the base (11) with two 12mm (½in) panel pins nailed through the top of the base, and sand smooth. Join the sides and string guide assembly to the base and secure in position from below with four 12mm (½in) countersunk screws.

4 Make the handle (13) from a 240mm (9½in) length of 8mm (⁵⁄₁₆in) birch dowel. Drill recessed holes for each of the animal strings, as shown on the plans.

5 Make the two handle collars (14) from 18mm (¾in) diameter circles of 9mm (⅜in) plywood. Drill a hole through the centre of each with a 9mm (⅜in) flat bit, cut out with a fretsaw and sand smooth. Drill a 1.2mm (³⁄₆₄in) hole in the side of each collar for the retaining pins, as shown.

6 Slide the collars onto the handle and ease the holes in the collars if necessary to ensure a sliding fit. Insert the handle and collars through the holes in the sides, making sure the collars are on the inside. Check that the handle spins freely in the holes with a small amount of play. Adjust the position of the shaft and collars so that the handle protrudes from each side by an equal amount. Secure the collars to the handle with the panel pins.

7 Glue a pair of animal supports (7) to each animal base (6), making sure that the slot between the supports is wide enough for the animal pieces. Place the supports with the straight grain of the ramin along the sides. Sand the base flush to the supports. Drill a hole for the string holder with a 2mm ($\frac{5}{64}$in) bit through the sides at the front of both supports.

8 Cut the nylon cord into five lengths of 1.5m (60in). Tie one end of each to a retainer made from a piece of cocktail stick inserted through the front hole in the animal supports, as shown. Trim and seal the ends with a lighted match to prevent fraying.

9 Hook the string guide and base assembly over the end of the bench or a large table. Place each animal in its support so that its front (nose or beak) aligns with the front of the support.

10 Drill two holes with a 2mm ($\frac{5}{64}$in) bit through each animal support with the animal in place, as shown. Line up the animals in their supports on the table top with the fronts of the supports close up against a spare piece of wood held down with weights to prevent movement. The distance between the edge of the table and the front of the weighted wood should be 1.3m (50in).

edge of bench

11 Thread the free ends of the strings through the string guide slots and then through the non-recessed side of the holes in the handle. Secure and adjust the length of each string as follows: pull the string taut; knot the end on the recessed side of the holes and insert cocktail sticks to secure, as shown; slide the knot down the string until it reaches the hole; trim end and seal with a lighted match; remove cocktail sticks. After all the strings are tied, check that they are of equal length and tension and adjust knots as necessary.

PAINTING AND FINISHING

12 Dismantle all non-glued parts. Remove the strings from the animal supports by pushing out the cocktail sticks. Apply two coats of white undercoat on both sides of the animals and banana tree, then paint as shown, leaving the edges unpainted. Paint the sides and string holder on both sides in shades of green. Paint the base in brownish greens. When the paint is dry, varnish all parts except the handle assembly. Allow to dry.

13 Cut cocktail sticks in half and insert in the holes to secure the animals in their supports. Secure the banana tree to one of the sides with two 12mm (½in) panel pins. Reassemble the other parts as before.

· BATHSUB ·

This jolly underwater craft is more than mere decoration – it actually works. Wind up the elastic band-driven propeller, put the submarine in the bath and watch it dive under the water just like a real submarine. It uses forward motion, ballast and a vane to control the depth and angle of the dive. This super toy will help your child learn about the principles of submarine technology while having fun in the bath (not to mention washing!).

EQUIPMENT

Coping saw

Junior hacksaw

Drill and bits
2mm ($\frac{5}{64}$in), 1.5mm ($\frac{1}{16}$in), 6.5mm ($\frac{1}{4}$in)

Soldering iron and solder

Tin snips

Scissors

Hammer

Glasspaper

Metal file

Round-nosed pliers

Diagonal cutters

Pair of compasses

Craft knife

MATERIALS

12mm ($\frac{1}{2}$in) birch plywood
180 × 62mm (7 × 2$\frac{1}{2}$in)

6.5mm ($\frac{1}{4}$in) birch dowel
50mm (2in)

4mm ($\frac{1}{8}$in) birch plywood
100 × 75mm (4 × 3in)

26 gauge brass sheet
50 × 50mm (2 × 2in)

1.5mm ($\frac{1}{16}$in) brass rod
75mm (3in)

Empty ball-point pen refill

150mm (6in) nail

1.2 × 75mm ($\frac{1}{16}$ × 3in) wide elastic bands
(×3)

12mm ($\frac{1}{2}$in) panel pins
(× 4)

Rapid-drying epoxy glue

Varnish

These are full size. Use the templates as positioning guides.

158MM (6¼")

40MM (1⅝")

②

6·5MM (¼") Ø

54MM (2⅛")

①

⑤

⑧

75MM
(3")

⑥

75MM (3")

7MM (5/16")

③

35MM (1⅜")

5MM (3/16")

73MM (2⅞")

2MM (5/64") Ø

④

12MM (½")

5MM (3/16")

Parts List

1. **Hull** 12mm ($\frac{1}{2}$in) birch plywood

2. **Conning tower** 4mm ($\frac{1}{8}$in) birch dowel

3. **Vane** 4mm ($\frac{1}{8}$in) birch plywood

4. **Propeller mount** 4mm ($\frac{1}{8}$in) birch plywood

5. **Propeller** 26g brass sheet

6. **Propeller shaft** 1.5mm ($\frac{1}{16}$in) brass rod

7. **Spacer** Empty ball-point pen refill

8. **Ballast** 150mm (6in) nail

1 Using templates traced from the diagrams, mark and cut out the plywood parts. Smooth the edges.

vertical

2 Secure the hull (1) in a vice, as shown. Using a 6.5mm (¼in) bit, drill the hole for the conning tower and ballast halfway through the hull, following the line on the template. Make sure that the drill remains parallel to the sides of the hull. Turn the hull around so that the base is uppermost and drill from this side until the two holes meet.

5 Check the fit of the dowel in the hole in the top of the hull. It should be tight but movable. Sand the end if necessary. Apply a generous amount of epoxy glue to the end of the dowel. Place in the hole to a depth of approximately 12mm ($\frac{1}{2}$in) and rotate to spread the glue around the hole. Spread the excess glue neatly around the join and stand the assembly vertically to dry. Then trim the dowel horizontally, as shown, to a length of 36mm (1$\frac{3}{8}$in).

glue

3 Drill the hole marked in the propeller mount (4) with a 2mm ($\frac{5}{64}$in) bit. Glue to the back end of the hull and secure with two panel pins, as shown.

MAKING THE PROPELLER

deburr

chamfer

4 Mark chamfer lines on the top (7mm $\frac{5}{16}$in) and underside (5mm $\frac{3}{16}$in) of the longer sides of the vane (3), as shown. Cut the chamfers carefully with a craft knife, paring away small amounts at a time. Check that the vane fits snugly under the hull. Trim further as necessary. When the chamfering is complete, smooth with glasspaper.

6 Draw the shape onto a piece of card and cut it out. Secure the card template onto the brass sheet with double-sided tape. Scribe the outline and the centre hole onto the metal with the compass point and remove the card. Drill the centre hole with a 1.5mm ($\frac{1}{16}$in) bit, and cut out the propeller with tin snips in stages, as shown. File off any burrs along the edges and polish with steel wool. Paint the shaded area of the prop in any matt colour, leaving a circle around the centre of about 6.5mm ($\frac{1}{4}$in). Leave to dry.

7 Assemble the propeller shaft (6) and the propeller so that the top of the propeller protrudes about 6.5mm (¼in). Drill a hole through a scrap of 12mm (½in) plywood. Insert the long end of the propshaft through the hole so that the propeller is supported by the plywood, and clamp the shaft in a vice.

9 Trim the end of the shaft with diagonal cutters so that it measures 45mm (1¾in) from the underside of the propeller. Using pliers, bend the end of the shaft to form a hook. This is best done in two stages, as shown.

8 Heat the soldering iron and then the propeller joint. Apply the solder, keeping the iron in place, until a neat blob of solder forms around the joint. The paint will keep the solder from flowing onto the propeller blades. If the joint does not form neatly, melt off the solder and try again. When the soldering is complete, wash off the paint and polish the propeller with metal polish.

10 Cut three 3mm (⅛in) sections with a craft knife from an empty ball-point pen refill for the propeller spacers and thread these onto the shaft.

11 Make a 30° template from a piece of scrap card as a guide to the angle to which to bend the propeller blades. These can be bent quite easily with your fingers to the shape shown.

12 Secure the nail (8) in a vice and use a hacksaw to cut it to a length of 54mm (2⅛in) from the head. File off any burrs.

13 Sand all the wooden parts smooth. Hold the hull on a sprue through the hole in the underside while you paint (see Basic Techniques). Paint the hull and vane with two coats in the background colour shown. Allow to dry and add the decoration to the hull. When all the paint is dry, apply three coats of varnish for a waterproof finish.

15 Insert the hook on the propeller shaft through the hole on the mount. Insert the ballast in the hole in the underside of the hull. Thread the three elastic bands over the end of the nail and propeller shaft. Wind for 30 turns clockwise and release, making sure that the propeller turns freely.

postcard both sides

waterline

vertical

14 Secure the hull in a vice, underside uppermost. Protect the paintwork with scrap card between the vice and hull. Scrape the paint off the hull and the top side of the vane where they are to be joined. Apply epoxy glue and secure in position with two panel pins.

16 Fill the bath with water to at least 305mm (12in) and launch the submarine. Check that it floats as shown and refer to the troubleshooting box if there is a problem.

17 Wind the propeller for 40 turns. Holding the propeller, place the submarine at one end of the bath and release. It should submerge and resurface at the other end. Refer to the troubleshooting box if there are problems. When all is working well, glue the ballast in position.

Fault	Cause	Remedy
Submarine too high in water	Too little ballast	Use longer length of nail
Submarine too low in water	Too much ballast	Trim nail 4mm ($\frac{1}{8}$in) at a time until the submarine floats correctly
Submarine goes forwards but does not dive	Too little power	Propeller not turned enough times
	Propeller movement impeded	Check that the hole in the propeller mount is large enough
	Hook not properly aligned	Rebend hook
	Angle of propeller blades too great or too small	Adjust angle of blades

· BIG FAT BIPLANE ·

Recapture the glamour of the early days of flying with this biplane. With decoration and detailing inspired by the aircraft of the 1930s and 40s, this model, with its turning propeller and rolling wheels, will be a big hit with young aircraft enthusiasts. Try personalizing the paintwork by substituting the number with that of the child's age, or by adding his or her name on the fuselage. Some parts of the plane are left unpainted to give the authentic impression of unbleached cotton, so be sure to choose knot-free wood with a pleasing grain.

EQUIPMENT

Fretsaw

Coping saw

Tenon saw

Plane

Drill and bits
6.5mm (¼in), 5mm (³/₁₆in)

Craft knife

Set square

Glasspaper and block

12mm (½in) chisel

Mallet

MATERIALS

22mm (⅞in) softwood
300 × 300mm
(12 × 12in)

4mm (⅛in) birch plywood
250 × 250mm
(10 × 10in)

6.5mm (¼in) birch dowel
300mm (12in)

12mm (½in) birch dowel
100mm (4in)

100mm (4in) nails
(× 2)

Scrap softwood
38 × 38 × 75mm
1½ × 1½ × 3in)

Scrap hard plastic or metal washers
(× 4)

Quick-drying epoxy glue

Paints

Varnish

Templates and Plans

All parts, including those in the side elevation, are reproduced at
50 percent, or 1:2.

Parts List

1. **Fuselage** 22mm (⅞in) softwood

2. **Spacer** 22mm (⅞in) softwood

3. **Top wing** 4mm (⅛in) birch plywood

4. **Top wing retaining dowels** (2) 6.5mm (¼in) birch dowel

5. **Bottom wing** 4mm (⅛in) birch plywood

6. **Bottom wing retaining dowels** (2) 6.5mm (¼in) birch dowel

7. **Undercarriage (right)** 16mm (⅝in) softwood

8. **Undercarriage (left)** 16mm (⅝in) softwood

9. **Undercarriage support** 4mm (⅛in) birch plywood

10. **Wheels** (2) 22mm (⅞in) softwood

11. **Wheel retainers** (2) 12mm (½in) birch dowel

12. **Axles** (2) Nail

13. **Wheel axle washers** (2) Hard plastic or metal

14. **Tail** 4mm (⅛in) birch plywood

15. **Rudder** 4mm (⅛in) birch plywood

16. **Engine** 22mm (⅞in) softwood

17. **Engine-retaining dowel** 6mm (¼in) birch dowel

18. **Engine and undercarriage retaining dowel** 6.5mm (¼in) birch dowel

19. **Propeller** 22mm (⅞in) softwood

20. **Propeller shaft** Nail

21. **Propeller shaft retainer** 12mm (½in) birch dowel

22. **Propeller shaft washers** (2) Hard plastic or metal

23. **Pilot head** Scrap softwood

24. **Nose** 6.5mm (¼in) birch dowel

25. **Neck** 12mm (½in) birch dowel

26. **Pilot-retaining dowel** 6.5mm (¼in) birch dowel

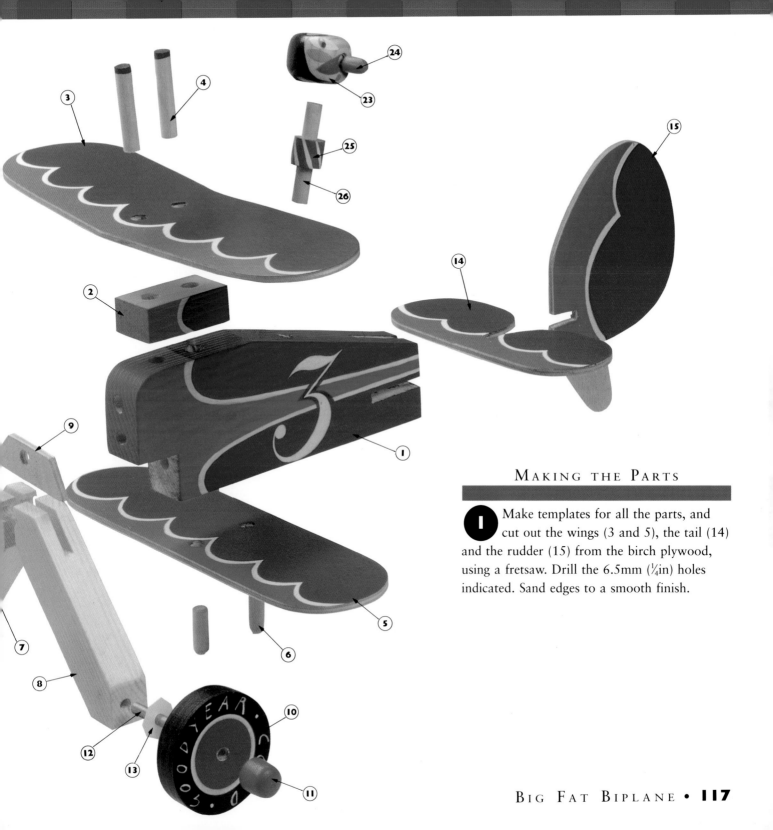

MAKING THE PARTS

1 Make templates for all the parts, and cut out the wings (3 and 5), the tail (14) and the rudder (15) from the birch plywood, using a fretsaw. Drill the 6.5mm (¼in) holes indicated. Sand edges to a smooth finish.

2 Using a craft knife, mark out the profile of the fuselage (1) on the softwood so that the grain runs horizontally. Allow an extra 6mm (¼in) at the front and back and an extra 1–2mm (⅟₁₆in) at the top and bottom. Cut out the basic shape with a tenon saw and plane along the grain to the exact size.

THE UNDERCARRIAGE

glue

3 Use medium glasspaper to smooth the end grain and to round off the front. Finish with fine glasspaper. Make slots in the tail end as shown.

4 Cut the two parts of the undercarriage (7 and 8) from 22mm (⅞in) softwood planed to 16mm (⅝in). Drill 4.5mm (¹¹⁄₆₄in) holes in one facet of one end of each piece to a depth of 16mm (⅝in), as shown. Make sure the holes are at right angles to the surface.

5 Glue the two pieces together on a flat surface to make the undercarriage.

7 Cut out the undercarriage support (9) from the 4mm (⅛in) plywood and glue this into the slot in the undercarriage. When dry, use a craft knife to trim the excess flush to the surface of the undercarriage. Sand smooth.

6 Secure the undercarriage in a vice and cut a 4mm (⅛in) slot across the top, by making two parallel cuts 18mm (¾in) deep and then removing the waste with a coping saw.

8 Drill a 6.5mm (¼in) hole through the centre of the assembly, as shown. Cut two 38mm (1½in) lengths from a 100mm (4in) nail, removing the head and point. Glue into the holes in the ends of the undercarriage.

9 Measure and cut the recess for the undercarriage in the fuselage, as shown.

10 With the undercarriage in position in its recess, supported in a vice by scrap softwood, drill through the hole in its centre into the fuselage to a depth of 12mm (½in). Cut two 50mm (2in) lengths of 6.5mm (¼in) birch dowel and insert one – the engine and undercarriage retainer (18) – into the hole. This should be a snug, but removable fit.

11 To make the engine (16), draw a circle with a radius of 30mm (1¼in) on the 22mm (⅞in) softwood. Cut out with a coping saw and drill the holes indicated. Smooth with fine glasspaper.

fuselage front

undercarriage

round off end

12 Position one of the larger holes in the engine over the dowel, and drill a hole through the second hole in the engine into the fuselage with a 6.5mm (¼in) bit to a depth of 12mm (½in). Insert the second 50mm (2in) long dowel. Using a 4.5mm (¹¹⁄₆₄in) bit, drill through the central hole into the fuselage. Insert but do not glue the propshaft (20) into this hole. Remove the engine and undercarriage from the fuselage and glue the two retaining dowels in place. Sand the ends flush to the engine.

13 Position the bottom wing (5) centred on the underside of the fuselage so that it is flush against the undercarriage. Drill through the existing holes in the wing into the fuselage to a depth of 12mm (½in). Apply glue inside the drilled holes and insert two 18mm (¾in) dowels to secure. Sand the protruding ends of the dowels to a rounded shape.

top wing

fuselage

14 Position the top wing (3) on the top of the fuselage, and drill through the existing holes into the fuselage with a 6.5mm (¼in) bit to a depth of 12mm (½in).

15 Make the wing spacer from a piece of softwood 45 × 14 × 28mm (1¾ × ⅝ × 1⅛in). Position this under the top wing and drill all the way through, using the two holes in the wing as a guide.

16 Mount the spacer in position on the fuselage with two 34mm (1⅜in) lengths of 6.5mm (¼in) dowel. Plane and sand the spacer flush to the sides of the fuselage, then remove the spacer, trim the ends and sand to finish. Glue the dowels into the spacer so that a short length protrudes to locate in the wing holes, and glue the spacer assembly to the top wing. Sand dowel ends flush to the wings.

17 Drill a hole for the pilot in the top of the fuselage using a 6.5mm (¼in) bit to a depth of 12mm (½in).

18 Shape the pilot's head from a scrap of softwood approximately 40 × 40 × 150mm (1½ × 1½ × 6in). Make saw cuts to a depth of 12mm (½in) around the piece along a line 30mm (1¼in) from one end, as shown. Make diagonal cuts on each side of the first cut and across the end of the piece. Use a craft knife to shape the head further and smooth with medium glasspaper. Cut the head from the spare wood and drill a hole for the neck and nose with a 6.5mm (¼in) bit. Cut a 25mm (1in) scrap of 6.5mm (¼in) dowel for the retainer.

19 Cut one 19mm (¾in) and two 10mm (⅜in) lengths of 12mm (½in) dowel for the propshaft retainer (21) and wheel retainers (11). Shape each piece as follows. Always wear thick gloves for this: insert a length of 100mm (4in) nail, from which you have removed the head, firmly into the exact centre of the dowel. Secure the free end of the nail in the drill chuck. Resting the drill on the bench and holding the end of the dowel against a pad of medium glasspaper, start the drill on slow. Using a turning action, sand the dowel end to a round shape.

MAKING THE PROPELLER

20 Plane a 100 × 50mm (4 × 2in) piece of 22mm (⅞in) softwood to a thickness of 10mm (⅜in). Draw two circles for the wheels (10) with a radius of 22mm (⅞in) and drill a hole in the centre of each with a 5mm (³⁄₁₆in) bit. Cut out with a fretsaw, as shown. Sand the rims, using the method described in step 19, but with a sanded-down piece of 6.5mm (¼in) dowel in place of the nail.

21 Mark out the propeller blank on a piece of softwood 22 × 150 × 16mm (⅞ × 6 × ⅝in), as shown. Drill the centre hole with a 5mm (³⁄₁₆in) bit.

24 Insert a length of 3mm (⅛in) wire rod through the hole in the propeller and support it as shown to check the balance. Sand further if necessary.

ASSEMBLY

sub-assembly 2

sub-assembly 1

22 Holding the blank in a vice at a slight angle, make the four angled cuts (marked A) with a tenon saw. With the propeller now secured horizontally at a slight angle, remove the rest of the unwanted wood (shaded in the illustration) with a chisel.

23 Shape the angled cuts into curves with a craft knife. Round off the ends with medium glasspaper and use fine sandpaper to smooth all edges.

25 Assemble all the parts to check the fit and that the propeller and wheels move easily on their shafts. Dismantle, paint and apply two coats of varnish.

26 Scrape any paint and varnish off surfaces to be glued to ensure good adhesion. Reassemble and glue with rapid-drying epoxy glue in the following order: undercarriage and engine to the fuselage; bottom wing, tail and rudder to fuselage; top wing and spacer to fuselage; propeller and wheels (unglued) onto their shafts with plastic or metal washers in place; propeller- and wheel-retainers to their shafts (insert card spacers to prevent glue getting on the propeller and wheels).

· SLITHERING SNAKE ·

Jointed snakes of this kind have a long pedigree. Often made in the East from bamboo or pithwood, this version uses the more easily obtainable softwood and ply. The subtle upward curve of the body produces a remarkably realistic snake-like movement.

EQUIPMENT

Tenon saw

Junior hacksaw

Fretsaw

Block plane

Set square

Round-nosed pliers

Diagonal cutters

Drill and bits
1.5mm (¹⁄₁₆in), 1.2mm
(³⁄₆₄in), 6.5mm (¼in)

Pin chuck

G-clamp

Glasspaper

Pair of compasses

MATERIALS

50 × 25mm (2 × 1in) PAR knot-free softwood
1.25m (50in)

4mm (⅛in) birch plywood
150 × 150mm (6 × 6in)

6.5mm (¼in) dowel
1500mm (60in)

1mm (³⁄₆₄in) welding wire
1m (39in)

Red plastic electric cable
50mm (2in)

40mm (1½in) panel pins
(× 2)

Toy-safe paints

Varnish

PVA wood glue

Postcard

The scale here for all parts is 80 percent, or 4:5.

1-13. **Body segments** Softwood

14. **Head** Softwood

15. **Tail** Softwood

16. **Tongue** Red electric cable

17. **Top joints (13)** 4mm (⅛in) birch plywood

18. **Bottom joints (13)** 4mm (⅛in) birch plywood

19. **Pivot shafts (14)** Welding wire

2 Make two marks 12mm (½in) apart in the centre of each end of the wood. Rule lines on the top and bottom sides of the wood from these marks to the edges of the middle segment as shown.

3 Secure the piece in a vice and plane down to the lines. Do not plane the middle segment.

MAKING THE SEGMENTS

1 Cut a 330 × 22mm (13 × ⅞in) piece of the softwood for the body segments (1–13). Along the top edge mark out thirteen 25mm (1in) divisions, as shown. Put an "x" in the middle one for reference and mark this segment on all sides of the wood.

4 Using a set square and the lines on the top edge as a guide, mark the rest of the segments on all sides of the piece. Mark the ends, and rule lines on the tapered sides of the wood from these marks to the edges of the middle segment, as shown. Secure in a vice and plane down to the marked lines as before.

5 Redraw the lines marking the segments that have been planed away. Along the centre of each side, draw two further parallel lines 9mm (⅜in) apart. Number the segments along one side for reference.

6 With the piece in a vice as before, plane along the corners to the level marked by the parallel lines. Be careful not to plane away the lines on the top and bottom.

7 Use a junior hacksaw with a sharp blade to separate the segments, following the ruled lines as accurately as possible. Lay a sheet of medium glasspaper on the bench, and sand both ends of each segment. Mark the centre of the sanded end of each segment. Drill through each one using a 6.5mm (¼in) bit.

MAKING THE JOINTS

The different hole spacing on the top and bottom sections gives the essential bias.

8 Mark out the plywood following the measurements on page 127 exactly. Use a card template to draw the curves. Mark the top joints (17) with a "t" and the bottom ones (18) with a "b". Use the point of a pair of compasses to prick the hole positions.

9 Drill the holes using a 1.2mm (³⁄₆₄in) bit. Using a fretsaw and mount, cut around the curves of each of the joints, and then cut between the curves to separate the joints. Smooth edges with fine glasspaper.

10 Glue each top joint to a body segment. Position the joints between the parallel lines on each body segment so that the segment is also between the guidelines marked on the joint. When the glue is dry, fix the bottom joints in the same way, so that the joints align as accurately as possible.

MAKING THE HEAD AND TAIL

11 Cut a 125mm (5in) piece of 50 ×
25mm (2 × 1in) softwood in half
lengthways to give two pieces measuring 125 ×
25 × 25mm (5 × 1 × 1in). Mark the shape of
the head on the top and sides of one of the
pieces, following the diagrams and
measurements shown on page 127.

14 Use the spare softwood for the tail,
marking out the sides as shown on page
127. Clamp the piece to the workbench and
remove the spare from the side with a tenon
saw. Plane smooth. Mark out the top of the tail
on the top surface and cut the shape as before.
Smooth the curved edges with glasspaper. Drill
a 1.2mm ($\frac{3}{64}$in) hole through the top of the tail
about 3–4mm ($\frac{1}{8}$in) from the front.

12 Holding the spare end of the wood in a
vice, use a tenon saw to cut the basic
head shape, following the marks. Cut off the
spare wood and use medium glasspaper to sand
the corners of the head to create a smooth,
rounded outline (see page 127).

PAINTING

13 Use a craft knife to chamfer the two
eye positions. Drill a 1.2mm ($\frac{3}{64}$in) hole
through the head 3–4mm ($\frac{1}{8}$in) from the base.
Drill a 1.5mm ($\frac{1}{16}$in) hole at an angle in the
underside of the head to a depth of 12mm ($\frac{1}{2}$in)
for the tongue (16).

15 Cut fifteen 100mm (4in) lengths of
6.5mm ($\frac{1}{4}$in) dowel to make sprues.
Chamfer both ends of 13 of these to a diameter
of 4mm ($\frac{1}{8}$in); these are the sprues for the body
segments. Drill a 1.5mm ($\frac{1}{16}$in) hole in one end
of the remaining two, and insert in each a
panel pin with the head snipped off. Chamfer
the other end as before; these are the sprues for
the head and tail. Make a holder by drilling
fifteen 6.5mm ($\frac{1}{4}$in) holes about 40mm ($1\frac{3}{4}$in)
apart in a piece of spare softwood.

bend

90°

17 Remove any paint clogging the pivot holes by redrilling. Cut the welding wire into fourteen 56mm (2¼in) lengths. Use round-nosed pliers to bend one end of each piece of wire into a loop 3–4mm (⅛in) in diameter, as shown.

16 After applying a white undercoat, paint all parts as shown, or design your own snake-like markings. Paint the background colour first and allow to dry before adding the markings in stages, as shown. To ensure that the pattern is the same on both sides of each segment, paint one side first and then turn the segment, keeping the sprue on the same side, and paint the other side exactly the same. When dry, apply two coats of varnish.

18 Lay out all the parts in their correct order. Although the numbers will be painted over, you should be able to judge this by their size. Make sure that the shorter top joints are on top.

19 Pass a pivot shaft through the holes in the joints between segments 1 and 2. Make a card template 11mm ($\frac{7}{16}$in) wide to measure the length of the protruding shaft. Trim with diagonal cutters to this length. Make a loop in the end as before, allowing 1.5mm ($\frac{1}{16}$in) clearance between the loop and the side of the joint. Continue to join all the segments in this way, finishing with the head and tail.

20 Tie a half-hitch knot in the red cable, as shown, and trim to length for the tongue. Use PVA wood glue to fix it into the hole in the underside of the head.

· PUFFIN ·

This "fertility" toy is a charming variation on the laying hens that were produced in Germany in the last century. The design is very popular with toddlers, who are intrigued by the way in which the eggs placed inside the puffin magically reappear when the body is pressed down. However, with young children it is advisable to keep this toy for special sessions of supervised play, to avoid the risk of rough handling damaging the bird or its mechanism.

MATERIALS

12mm (½in) birch plywood
100 × 100mm (4 × 4in)

9mm (⅜in) birch plywood
300 × 300mm (12 × 12in)

4mm (⅛in) birch plywood
300 × 300mm (12 × 12in)

1.5mm (¹⁄₁₆in) birch plywood
500 × 100mm (20 × 4in)

6.5mm (¼in) birch dowel
610mm (24in)

1.5mm (¹⁄₁₆in) brass rod
75mm (3in)

2.5mm (³⁄₃₂in) brass rod
150mm (6in)

20 and 22g piano wire
150mm (6in)

22g brass sheet
75 × 75mm (3 × 3in)

Scrap softwood

Tinplate from oil can
100 × 50mm (4 × 2in)

25mm (1in) birch/balls
(× 5)

40mm (1½in) countersunk screws
(× 2)

12mm (½in) countersunk screws
(× 2)

12mm (½in) panel pins

Toy-safe paints

PVA wood glue or rapid-drying epoxy resin

Dressmaker's pins

Car-body filler

EQUIPMENT

Fretsaw

Tenon saw

Drill and bits
1mm (³⁄₆₄in), 1.5mm (¹⁄₁₆in), 2.5mm (³⁄₃₂in), 3mm (⁷⁄₆₄in) 5mm (³⁄₁₆in), 6.5mm (¼in)

Pin chuck

Tin snips

Rasp or coarse glasspaper and dowel

Soldering iron and solder

Diagonal cutters

Craft knife

Glasspaper

TEMPLATES AND PLANS

The body surround (part 3) is 25 percent, or 1:4. The other parts are at 50 percent.

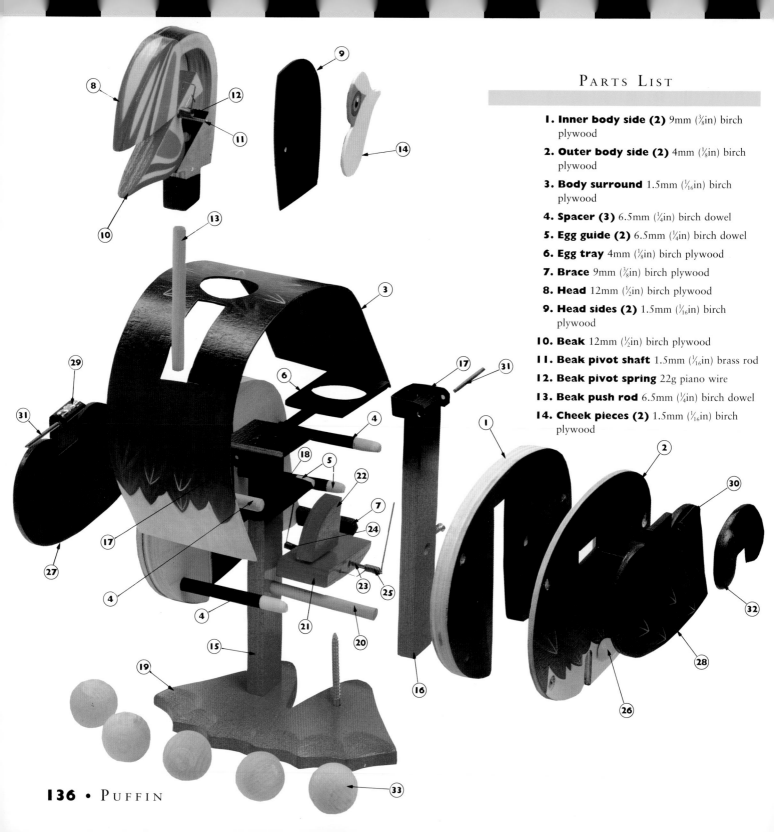

1. Inner body side (2) 9mm (⅜in) birch plywood

2. Outer body side (2) 4mm (⅛in) birch plywood

3. Body surround 1.5mm (1/16in) birch plywood

4. Spacer (3) 6.5mm (¼in) birch dowel

5. Egg guide (2) 6.5mm (¼in) birch dowel

6. Egg tray 4mm (⅛in) birch plywood

7. Brace 9mm (⅜in) birch plywood

8. Head 12mm (½in) birch plywood

9. Head sides (2) 1.5mm (1/16in) birch plywood

10. Beak 12mm (½in) birch plywood

11. Beak pivot shaft 1.5mm (1/16in) brass rod

12. Beak pivot spring 22g piano wire

13. Beak push rod 6.5mm (¼in) birch dowel

14. Cheek pieces (2) 1.5mm (1/16in) birch plywood

15. **Leg (right)** 9mm (⅜in) birch plywood

16. **Leg (left)** 9mm (⅜in) birch plywood

17. **Wing pivot shaft bearings (2)** 22g brass sheet

18. **Beak push rod plate** 22g brass sheet

19. **Feet** 9mm (⅜in) birch plywood

20. **Egg door push rod** 6.5mm (¼in) birch dowel

21. **Egg door** 9mm (⅜in) birch plywood

22. **Egg stop** 9mm (⅜in) birch plywood

23. **Egg door pivot shaft** 2.5mm (³⁄₃₂in) brass rod

24. **Egg door spring (right)** 20g piano wire

25. **Egg door spring (left)** 20g piano wire

26. **Egg door pivot shaft retainers (2)** Softwood

27. **Wing (right)** 4mm (⅛in) birch plywood

28. **Wing (left)** 4mm (⅛in) birch plywood

29. **Wing bearing (right)** Tinplate

30. **Wing bearing (left)** Tinplate

31. **Wing pivot shaft (2)** 2.5mm (³⁄₃₂in) brass rod

32. **Wing pivot shaft retainers (2)** 9mm (⅜in) birch plywood

33. **Eggs (5)** 25mm (1in) birch balls

MAKING THE PARTS

1 Trace the templates and cut out the parts in the materials indicated using a fretsaw and tenon saw. Drill the marked holes in the bit size specified. When making two parts from the same template, tack or tape two sheets of plywood together and cut both pieces at the same time. Cut the head and beak pieces (8 and 10) as one piece and shape the front of the beak to a rounded point before separating them by cutting along the marked line.

4 Cut the birch dowel to the lengths specified in the table. Sand, if necessary, so that the pieces fit snugly in the 6.5mm (¼in) holes drilled in the body pieces.

Part (number)	Length
4. Spacers (× 3)	70mm (2¾in)
5. Egg guides (× 2)	50mm (2in)
20. Egg door push rod (× 1)	64mm (2½in)
13. Beak push rod (× 1)	60mm (2⅜in)

2 To ensure correct alignment of the holes in the inner (1) and outer (2) body pieces, tack these together in pairs with panel pins and drill through both pieces together. With the two outer body pieces tacked or taped together in a vice, shape the two outside edges of the wing pivot holes using a craft knife. Finish with glasspaper.

clockwise

anticlockwise

5 Hold a 2.5mm (³⁄₃₂in) drill bit in a vice and make the beak pivot spring (12) and egg door springs (24 and 25) by winding piano wire around the bit shank in the directions shown for the spcified number of turns. When each spring is complete, remove from the bit and trim the ends to the required length and bend to the shape illustrated.

3 Shape the toes of the feet piece (19) with a rasp or coarse glasspaper wrapped around a 25mm (1in) dowel.

6 Use tin snips to cut out the brass sheet for two wing pivot shaft bearings (17). Then cut out the beak push rod plate (18), and drill the 1.2mm ($\frac{3}{64}$in) holes in all pieces, as indicated on the templates.

THE BODY CAVITY

The works and the chamber for the eggs are enclosed in a cavity between the inner and outer body side pairings and the surround.

7 Chamfer both ends of the three spacers and insert them in the holes on the inner side of one inner body piece (1) so that the ends protrude by 5mm ($\frac{3}{16}$in). Apply glue to the sides and underside of the egg tray (6), as shown, and position over the top spacers. Place the other inner body piece over the spacers so that the ends protrude as before. Make sure that the sides are parallel.

8 Chamfer one end of each egg guide. When the glue is dry, insert the egg guides in the remaining holes in the inner body pieces by pushing them, chamfered end first, from one side.

9 Apply glue to the outer surface of each inner body piece. Thread each outer body piece (2) over the protruding ends of the spacers of the corresponding inner body piece, making sure that the rounded side of the slot of each outer body piece is facing outwards. Secure with panel pins, supporting the assembly with scrap wood or over the corner of your workbench. Allow to dry, then cut off the protruding ends of the spacers on the outer sides of the body and sand smooth.

glue
surface

glue
surface

nail

glue
surface

10 Position the body surround (3) so that the centre of the egg hole in the surround lines up with the point marked on the outer body pieces (2). When you are happy with the positioning, apply glue to the edges of the body pieces and secure the surround to the body with panel pins. Cut the tail brace (7) from scrap 9mm (⅜in) birch plywood and glue between the body sides at the tail end.

11 When the whole assembly is dry, trim the surround flush with the body sides and tail with a craft knife and sand smooth.

MAKING THE HEAD

The head assembly is bold and bright and features a spring-loaded lower half to give the highly entertaining "squawking" effect.

12 Drill a hole vertically through the centre of the "neck" of the head (8), using a 6.5mm (¼in) bit. Glue one head side (9) to one side of the head, allowing the edges of the head side to protrude at the top and back of the head to allow for trimming later.

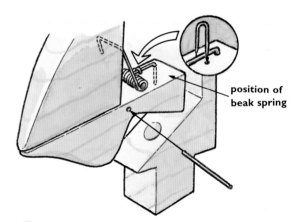

position of
beak spring

13 Position the beak (10) inside the head. Using the existing hole in the beak as a guide, drill through the head side using a 1.5mm (¹⁄₁₆in) bit. Press one end of the beak pivot spring (12) into the beak, as shown, and secure with a bent dressmaker's pin. Insert the 1.5mm (¹⁄₁₆in) rod for the beak pivot shaft (11) through the holes in the beak and head side.

14 Insert the beak push rod (13) into the neck hole and check that it slides up and down freely, and that the beak opens and closes satisfactorily. Remove the beak and attach the other head side with glue. When dry, drill through the assembly with a 1.5mm ($\frac{1}{16}$in) bit to make the beak pivot hole. Trim the edges, sand and then insert the beak mechanism and test the movement again.

15 Remove the beak and push rod. Slot the head assembly through the rectangular hole in the body to locate in the square hole in the egg tray and glue to secure. When dry, fill any gaps between head and body with car-body filler.

THE MAIN MECHANISM

This assembly connects the wings with the legs and is also spring-loaded to make the wings flap when the bird is pressed down.

16 Making sure that the screw holes in each leg are facing the right way, use panel pins to secure the two wing pivot shaft bearings (17) to the tops of the legs in the position indicated on the template. File off the points of the nails, if they protrude.

17 Drill holes in each end of the bearings with a 2.5mm ($\frac{3}{32}$in) bit, at a point 17mm ($1\frac{1}{16}$in) from the edge of the wood. Snip off the corners of the bearings. Bend the sides of the bearings up, flush to the sides of the legs

18 Bend the beak push rod plate (8) along the line marked on the template into a 90° angle. Secure with panel pins to the right leg (15) in the position shown on the template. Smooth all brass edges with a file.

19 With a 2.5mm (³⁄₃₂in) drill bit in a vice, coil one end of each wing bearing (29 and 30) around the shank three times with a pair of pliers. Bend each bearing to form a right angle at a point 20mm (³⁄₄in) from the base of the coil.

level →

20 Insert one of the bearings through the slot in one of the wings (27) and repeat this with the other wing from the opposite side. Working on each wing in turn in a vice, bend the bearings upwards and coil the free end around the drill bit as before, until it is level with the coil at the other end. Solder the coils together. File metal edges smooth.

21 Refit the beak parts and beak push rod. Insert the right leg (15) inside the body with the wing pivot shaft bearings protruding through the slot in the body and check that the beak push rod moves up and down when you push the leg. You may need to trim the push rod a little. Insert the left leg (16) and attach the feet with the 40mm (1½in) screws.

22 Glue the egg stop (22) to the egg door (21). Make the egg door pivot shaft (23) from a 60mm (2⅜in) length of 2.5mm (³⁄₃₂in) brass rod and thread this through the egg door. Place each egg door spring (24 and 25) over the ends of the shaft. Press the bent ends of each spring into the sides of the door.

23 Remove the shaft, leaving the springs attached, and position the door between the legs, as shown. Insert the pivot shaft through the hole in one of the body sides, through the springs and door, and out through the other body side. Holding back the egg door, insert the egg door push rod (20) through the slot in the body sides and through the holes in both legs.

24 The egg door should now open when you push the legs. Put the five eggs (33) into the round hole in the top of the body, and press the bird down. An egg should come out of the egg door each time you do this. If you are happy with the way it works, secure the egg door push rod between the legs with the 12mm (½in) screws inserted in the horizontal holes in the backs of the legs. Make sure that the sides of the legs do not rub against the body.

25 Cut two 29mm (1⅛in) lengths of 2.5mm (³⁄₃₂in) brass rod for the wing pivot shafts (31) and insert them through the wing pivot shaft bearings and the hole formed by the outer coil of the wing bearings. Check the troubleshooting box before painting.

26 Remove the following parts: wing pivot shafts; egg door pivot shaft; leg and feet screws; legs; egg door; beak pivot shaft; beak and beak push rod. Shape the wing pivot shaft retainers (32) with a craft knife and coarse glasspaper as shown. Finish with fine glasspaper. Make two egg door pivot shaft retainers (26) from scrap softwood in the same way. Paint and varnish all parts to a hard-wearing finish (see Basic Techniques).

27 Reassemble when dry, adding the cheek pieces (14). After assembling the wings, glue the wing pivot shaft retainers and egg door pivot shaft retainers into position. Cover the screw holes with scrap dowel cut and sanded flush to the surface, and touch up the paintwork if necessary.

TROUBLESHOOTING

Fault	Cause	Remedy
Very stiff action	Legs rubbing against body	Reposition legs closer together
Eggs not coming down	Egg stop too big	Trim egg stop
Eggs jam inside	Egg stop too small	Remake larger
Puffin stops in "down position" (see fault 1)	Springs too weak; wings jamming	Increase strength of spring by bending; check wing bearings
Puffin hard to press down (see fault 1)	Springs too strong	Decrease strength of spring by bending
Beak opens too far or not enough	Beak push rod too short or too long	Trim or remake longer

· LION TAMER ·

This fascinating toy, based on a circus scene in which a lion tamer places his head inside a lion's mouth, is a simple automaton – a model with moving parts. In this case the movement is produced by turning a handle which moves the interconnecting cog wheels and cams that turn the lion tamer and the lion. Toys of this kind need to be handled with care, and are probably unsuitable for small children to play with unsupervised. The cog-wheel principle can be adapted for use in automata of your own design.

EQUIPMENT

Fretsaw

Tenon saw

Drill and bits
1.2mm (³⁄₆₄in),
1.5mm (¹⁄₁₆in),
2.5mm (³⁄₃₂in),
6.5mm (¼in)

Pin chuck

Pair of compasses

Protractor

Diagonal cutters

Metal file

Small G-clamp

Needle- and round-nosed pliers

Screwdriver

Craft knife

MATERIALS

4mm (⅛in) hardboard
200 × 150mm
(8 × 6in)

9mm (⅜in) birch plywood
150 × 150mm
(6 × 6in)

4mm (⅛in) birch plywood
150 × 150mm
(6 × 6in)

1.5mm (¹⁄₁₆in) birch plywood
75 × 50mm
(3 × 2in)

22mm (⅞in) softwood
150 × 150mm
(6 × 6in)

6.5mm (¼in) birch dowel
305mm (12in)

1.5mm (¹⁄₁₆in) birch dowel
75mm (3in)

1.5mm (¹⁄₁₆in) copper-coated welding rod
150mm (6in)

1mm (¹⁄₃₂in) welding wire or brass rod
305mm (12in)

Clear plastic sheet
25 × 25mm
(1 × 1in)

12mm (½in) gimp or panel pins
18g (½oz)

12mm (½in) screws
(× 6)

18mm (¾in) brass or mild steel panel pins
18g (½oz)

Dressmaking pins
(× 2)

Toy-safe paints

Varnish

Rapid-drying epoxy glue

Scrap plywood
75 × 75mm
(3 × 3in)

Scrap hardboard

Templates and Plans

The templates on this page are shown at 80 percent, or 4:5. The side elevation and templates on the following pages are full size.

2·5mm (³/₃₂") ∅

16mm (⁵/₈") ∅

1mm (³/₆₄") ∅

①

7mm (⁹/₃₂") ∅

2·5mm (³/₃₂") ∅

2·5mm (³/₃₂") ∅

②

7mm (⁹/₃₂") ∅

③

7mm (⁹/₃₂") ∅

④

6·5mm (¹/₄") ∅

⑨

6·5mm (¼") ⌀

6·5mm (¼") ⌀

6·5mm (¼") ⌀

6·5mm (¼") ⌀

1·5mm (¹/₁₆") ⌀

6·5mm (¼") ⌀

3·2mm (⅛") ⌀

1·5mm (¹/₁₆") ⌀

6·5mm (¼") ⌀

1·5mm (¹/₁₆") ⌀

1mm (³/₆₄") ⌀

1·5mm (¹/₁₆") ⌀

1mm (³/₆₄") = ⌀

1mm (³/₆₄") ⌀

1mm (³/₆₄") ⌀

6·5mm (¼") ⌀

PARTS LIST

1. **Platform** Hardboard

2. **Base** Hardboard

3. **Side panels** (2) 9mm ($\frac{3}{8}$in) birch plywood

4. **Tamer stand** Softwood

5. **Main shaft** 6.5mm ($\frac{1}{4}$in) birch dowel

6. **Handle** 9mm ($\frac{3}{8}$in) birch plywood

7. **Handle shaft** 6.5mm ($\frac{1}{4}$in) birch dowel

8. **Tamer cam** 9mm ($\frac{3}{8}$in) birch plywood

9. **Cog** (2) 4mm ($\frac{1}{8}$in) birch plywood

10. **Lion cam** 9mm ($\frac{3}{8}$in) birch plywood

11. **Collar** (3) 9mm ($\frac{3}{8}$in) birch plywood

12. **Hollow shaft** 6.5mm ($\frac{1}{4}$in) birch dowel

13. **Cam follower** Scrap plywood

14. **Cam follower rod** 1.5mm ($\frac{1}{16}$in) metal rod

15. **Spacer** 4mm ($\frac{1}{8}$in) birch plywood

16. **Tamer base** Softwood

17. **Tamer leg** (2) 4mm ($\frac{1}{8}$in) birch plywood

18. **Tamer body** Softwood

19. Tamer coat-tails 1.5mm (1/16in) birch plywood

20. Tamer right arm 4mm (1/8) birch plywood

21. Tamer left arm 4mm (1/8in) birch plywood

22. Tamer neck 6.5mm (1/4in) birch dowel

23. Tamer head Softwood

24. Tamer nose Scrap 1.5mm (1/16in) dowel

25. Tamer pivot shaft 1.5mm (1/16in) metal rod

26. Lion body Softwood

27. Lion jaw Softwood

28. Lion head Softwood

29. Lion nose Scrap 6.5mm (1/4in) dowel

30. Lion ear (2) 1.5mm (1/16in) birch plywood

31. Lion side (2) 4mm (1/8in) birch plywood

32. Lion tail 4mm (1/8in) birch plywood

33. Lion push rod Scrap 6.5mm (1/4in) dowel

34. Lion jaw pivot shaft 1.5mm (1/16in) metal rod

35. Lion head stay 1mm (3/64in) wire

36. Lion head stay retainer (2) 1mm (3/64in) wire

37. Lion pivot shaft 1mm (3/64in) wire

MAKING THE PARTS

Because of the complexity of the mechanism, take great care with the accuracy of the parts.

1 Trace the templates and mark each element, including the drill holes, on the type of wood indicated. Cut out all the pieces. Shape the softwood parts with a plane and sand all parts smooth. Drill the holes.

2 Cut the 6.5mm (1/4in) dowel to the following lengths: 180mm (7in); 54mm (2 1/8in); 50mm (2in); 35mm (1 3/8in); 22mm (7/8in); 9mm (3/8in). See the side elevation.

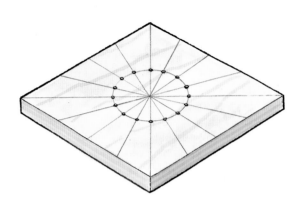

3 To make the cogs (9), first make a jig using a 100mm (4in) square of scrap plywood. Find the centre as shown and draw a circle with a diameter of 42mm (1¹¹⁄₁₆in). Mark out 16 radiating lines at 22.5° angles and drill holes in the positions indicated.

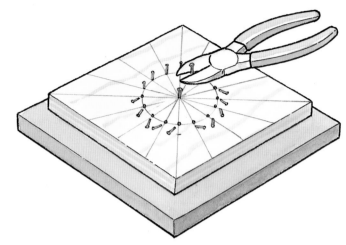

5 Hammer panel pins through the marked points on the jig and cog blank so that they protrude about 1.5mm (¹⁄₁₆in) into the hardboard. Clip off the heads of the pins close to the jig with diagonal cutters. Remove the centre pin and gently separate the cog from the jig.

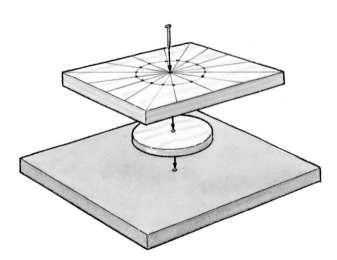

4 Attach a cog blank (9) underneath the jig, using an 18mm (¾in) brass panel pin through the centre of the jig and cog blank and onto a scrap of hardboard.

6 Drill the centre hole of the cog with a 6.5mm (¼in) bit and file the points of the cog pins smooth on the underside.

7 Push the main shaft (5) through the cog and glue the cog halfway along. Position a collar (11) behind the cog, and secure with an 18mm (¾in) panel pin through the collar.

8 Place the tamer cam (8) on the shaft. Align the bottom of the cam with one of the cog teeth and mark the cog in pencil, as shown. Retain the cam with a gimp pin.

9 Position the lion cam (10) as shown and place the two end collars on the shaft. A tight but movable fit is important. Do not secure them, as they may need adjusting.

10 Make the second cog using the jig as before, and glue the hollow shaft (12) at right angles to the centre of the cog, flush to the underside (see elevation).

11 Nail the stand (4) to the top of the platform where shown, using three gimp pins. Make sure the centre hole of the stand aligns accurately with the hole in the platform.

LION TAMER • **153**

12 Insert the hollow shaft with cog attached through the hole in the platform and retain in position with the spacer (15), which should be a tight but movable fit. The cog and shaft should spin freely.

14 Insert the tamer cam follower rod (14) through the hole in the tamer cam follower (13) and glue. Place the rod through the hollow shaft (12).

15 Screw the platform to the side panels, making sure the rod does not fall out of the shaft, by holding it with fingers.

13 Place the side panels (3) of the stand on the main shaft and screw these to the base (2) as indicated. Make sure that the shaft spins freely. Slot pieces 6 and 7 together to make the handle and place on the end of the shaft, aligned to the tamer cam, as shown.

16 Mark on the tamer cog where it meets the pencil mark on the drive cog.

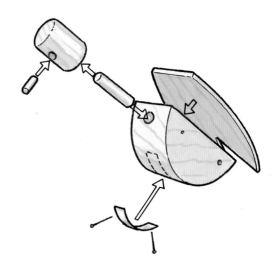

17 Make the jig for aligning the tamer's legs using a piece of 1.5mm (¹⁄₁₆in) dowel or wire rod fixed at right angles into a hole drilled in scrap 9mm (³⁄₈in) plywood.

19 Glue the tamer's coat-tails (19) to the body (18), the neck (22) to the head (23) and the nose (24) to the head. Position the head on the body. Attach the piece of plastic to the body as shown with dressmaking pins trimmed to about 6.5mm (¼in).

18 Nail the tamer's right leg (17) to the tamer base (16) using two gimp pins. Place the assembly on the jig so that the rod passes through the hole in the leg. Position the left leg as shown and nail to the base. Remove the leg assembly from the jig.

20 Attach the arms (20 and 21) with gimp pins, making sure (21) is on the left. Place the body between the leg assembly and thread the tamer pivot shaft (25) through the legs and body. Ensure that the parts swivel smoothly on the shaft.

21 Glue the lion's lower jaw (27) to the lion's body (26). Drill two holes in the back of the lion's head, slightly to the left as shown, with a 1mm ($\frac{3}{64}$in) bit. Glue the ears (30) and the nose (29) to the head.

23 Thread the jaw pivot shaft (34) through the head pivot hole. Align the sides (31) on the shaft. Stand the assembly on a flat surface to ensure that the lower pivot holes also align. When positioned correctly, nail each side to the body with two gimp pins.

22 Clamp the head to the jaw, using a piece of thin card as a spacer between to ensure a good "snap" when the jaws open and close.

24 Glue the tail (32) in position, making sure it doesn't cover the push rod hole, and position the push rod (33).

CHECKING THE ASSEMBLY

25 Turn the handle of the main drive to the up position and then turn it so that the pencil marks are at opposite ends, as shown. Place the tamer assembly over the hollow shaft facing the handle end of the platform. Check that the tamer revolves properly and that he bends down as you turn the handle to the up position. You may need to unscrew the platform and shorten the cam follower rod to achieve this. When you are satisfied with the length, sand the top of the rod so that it is smooth and rounded.

26 Thread the lion pivot shaft (37) through the holes in its feet and bend the ends down as shown. Place the lion on the platform with the push rod passing through the hole in the platform so that it touches the lion cam. Pass the ends of the lion pivot shaft through the holes in the platform as shown and bend to secure.

27 Make up the head stay (35) and the two head stay retainers (36) from the 1mm (¹⁄₃₂in) wire. Bend the ends of the head stay as shown so that its length is 68m (2¾in). The head stay retainers are each approximately 40mm (1½in) long. Bend one of the head stay retainers into a U-shape, insert the ends into the holes in the back of the lion's head and push in firmly. Loop the squared end of the head stay through the retainer. Bend the second retainer into a U-shape. Attach it to the other end of the head stay and insert it through the holes in the platform, bending the ends underneath to secure.

28 Check the timing of the mechanism. Adjust the tamer movement by rotating him on the hollow shaft. He should start to bend down when the handle reaches the 8 o'clock position and should be fully bent down and facing the lion at 12 o'clock. The lion should begin to open his mouth when the handle is at 7 o'clock; the mouth is fully open at 12 o'clock and snaps shut at 1 o'clock. Fine tune the timing by adjusting the position of the lion cam on the main shaft. Check the troubleshooting box before painting.

TROUBLESHOOTING

Fault	Cause	Remedy
Handle hard to turn	Main shaft bearing holes too small; not enough clearance between collars and sides	Ease out with round file; reposition collars
Stiff cog action	Cogs not meshing properly; nails not straight	Try different mesh position; straighten nails
Tamer's head hits lion's·head	Tamer bending down too far	Put pin stop in tamer body side to stop against leg
Tamer out of sync with lion	Tamer in wrong position on hollow shaft; lion cam in wrong position on main shaft	Readjust positions
Lion coming too far or not forward enough	Lion push rod too short or too long	Readjust length of push rod
Lion's mouth opens too little or too much	Head stay too long or too short	Adjust length of head stay

PAINTING AND FINISHING

When you are satisfied with the assembly, mark the positions of all the adjustable parts and dismantle the assembly (apart from nailed and glued items). You will need to unscrew the platform.

29 Paint and varnish the parts individually as desired, except the works. Give all painted parts two coats of matt white, sanding down between coats. The speckled appearance on the lion's head and body is achieved by flicking first brown and then cream paint with a toothbrush over a yellow ochre undercoat. When the head is dry, paint the eyes, nose and teeth. The lion is not varnished. When all parts are dry, reassemble, securing the adjustable parts with glue and panel pins.

· OFF-ROAD VEHICLE ·

Wheeled toys of all kinds are always popular, but the play value of this sturdy vehicle is enhanced by sophisticated features such as its independent suspension system, working winch and flashing warning light. The contrasting colours of the unpainted dark Far East plywood and the pale birch plywood and dowel, together with the green painted bodywork contribute to the rugged look of this versatile vehicle.

MATERIALS

12mm (½in) Far East plywood
610 × 305mm
(24 × 12in)

12mm (½in) birch plywood
305 × 150mm
(12 × 6in)

6.5mm (¼in) birch dowel
610mm (24in)

12mm (½in) birch dowel
305mm (12in)

Clear perspex or acrylic sheet
100 × 75mm (4 × 3in)

150mm (6in) nails (×4)

Galvanized roofing nut and bolt
6 × 90mm (¼ ×3½in)

Nylon cord
2m (7ft)

10mm (⅜in) flashing yellow LED (light-emitting diode)

Miniature push-button switch

9v battery (PP3) with connector and leads

High pressure bicycle inner tube
150 × 32mm (6 × 1¼in)

Rapid-drying epoxy glue

Toy-safe paints

25mm (1in) panel pins (× 20)

Dressmaker's pins

Masking tape

Cardboard

EQUIPMENT

Fretsaw

Tenon saw

Hacksaw

57mm (2¼in) hole saw

Drill and bits
6.5mm (¼in), 1.5mm (¹⁄₁₆in), 5.5mm (⁷⁄₃₂in), 3.3mm (⅛in), 5mm (³⁄₁₆in)
Flat bits: 12mm (½in), 9mm (⅜in)
Countersink bit

12mm (½in) chisel

Craft knife

5mm (⁵⁄₁₆in) round file

Soldering iron and solder

Diagonal cutters

Pliers

Pair of compasses

Hammer

Rasp

TEMPLATES AND PLANS

The parts on this and the following page are at 50 percent, or 1:2. Those
on page 163 are full size.

70MM (2¾")

6·5MM (¼") Ø
⑤ 6MM (¹³⁄₆₄") Ø

9MM
(3/8")

9MM
(3/8")

9MM
(3/8")

9MM
(3/8")

45MM (1¾")

6·5MM (¼") Ø
⑥
6MM (¹⁵⁄₆₄") Ø

9MM
(3/8")

9MM
(3/8")

5·6MM (⁷⁄₃₂") Ø

⑪

16MM (⅝")

㊲
2 × 1·6MM
(¹⁄₁₆") Ø

6·5MM
(¼")

6·5MM (¼") Ø
⑫

25MM
(1")

56MM (2¼")

32MM (1¼")

CA 53421

⑭

64MM (2½")

6·5MM
(¼")
Ø
④

27MM (1³⁄₁₆")

6·5MM
(¼") Ø
⑨

16MM (⅝")

6·5MM (¼") Ø
⑩

1·6MM
(¹⁄₁₆") Ø

12MM
(½") Ø
㉗

1·6MM
(¹⁄₁₆") Ø

12MM
(½") Ø
㉘

3·2MM
(⅛")
Ø

1·6MM
(¹⁄₁₆") Ø
�34

30

6·5MM
(¼") Ø

29

3·2MM (⅛") Ø

�33

1. Chassis (2) Far East plywood

2. Suspension arm axle (2) Nail

3. Chassis band dowel (2) 6.5mm (¼in) birch dowel

4. Chassis spacers (4) 12mm (½in) birch dowel

5. Long suspension arm (4) Far East plywood

6. Short suspension arm Far East plywood

7. Suspension band dowel (4) 6.5mm (¼in) birch dowel

8. Stub axle (4) Nail

9. Stub axle spacer (4) 12mm (½in) birch dowel

10. Wheel (4) 12mm (½in) birch plywood

11. Wheel retainer (4) 12mm (½in) birch plywood

12. Clamp Far East plywood

13. Bolt Galvanized roofing bolt

14. Number plate Far East plywood

15. Bands (4) Bicycle inner tube

16. Floor Far East plywood

17. Sides (2) Far East plywood

18. Skirt (2) Far East plywood

19. Beam Far East plywood

20. Cab base Far East plywood

21. Cab window frame (2) 12mm (½in) birch plywood

22. Cab roof Far East plywood

23. Windscreen Perspex/acrylic sheet

24. Bonnet Far East plywood

25. Pick-up front and back (2) Far East plywood

26. Winch shaft 12mm (½in) birch dowel

27. **Winch ratchet** 12mm (½in) birch plywood

28. **Winch end** 12mm (½in) birch plywood

29. **Winch pawl** 12mm (½in) birch plywood

30. **Winch pawl handle** 6.5mm (¼in) birch dowel

31. **Winch pawl shaft** 6.5mm (¼in) birch dowel

32. **Winch cord** Nylon cord

33. **Winch hook** 12mm (½in) birch plywood cut to 6.5mm (¼in)

34. **Winch cord guide** 12mm (½in) birch plywood

35. **Tow hook** 6.5mm (¼in) birch dowel

36. **Light** Yellow flashing LED

37. **Light holder** 12mm (½in) birch dowel

38. **Switch**

39. **Battery**

40. **Battery connector and wire**

41. **Nut**

MAKING THE CHASSIS

1 Make templates for all parts indicated, and mark the positions of all the drill holes. Cut out all the parts in the type of wood indicated.

2 Fix the two chassis pieces (1) together with panel pins and drill the four holes indicated with a 6.5mm (¼in) bit. Cut the two suspension arm axles (2) from two 150mm (6in) nails to a length of 96mm (3¾in) and two chassis band dowels (3) from 6.5mm (¼in) birch dowel to a length of 90mm (3½in).

3 File the ends of the metal axles to remove any sharp edges. Paint the chassis sides black all over, and allow to dry.

4 Rest one of the chassis sides over a vice, as shown, using cardboard to protect the paintwork, and hammer the axles and dowels into the holes in one chassis side, as shown, so the axle ends protrude by 25mm (1in) and the dowel ends by 19mm (¾in).

5 From the 12mm (½in) birch dowel, cut four lengths of 21mm (1³⁄₁₆in) for the chassis spacers (4). Drill a hole through the centre of each with a 6.5mm (¼in) bit. Paint black, and allow to dry. Put the spacers on the axles and dowels on the inside of the chassis. Hammer on the other chassis side so that the assembly is tight and the axle and dowel ends protrude by an equal amount on both sides.

MAKING THE SUSPENSION ARMS

6 Drill holes in the long and short elements of the suspension arms (5 and 6) as indicated on the template.

7 Make a jig by hammering part of a 150mm (6in) nail through the centre of a 76 × 76mm (3 × 3in) piece of scrap plywood. Cut the head off the nail, which should protrude by 38mm (1½in).

8 Place one long suspension arm (5) on the jig with one of the holes over the nail. Then glue a short suspension arm (6) on top at 90° to the long arm. Drill two pilot holes through the short suspension arm with a 1.5mm (1/16in) bit and hammer two panel pins through both pieces. Remove from jig and file off the points of the pins if they protrude.

9 Assemble the remaining suspension arm pieces in the same way, ensuring that you make two assemblies with the short piece projecting to the right and two projecting to the left. Varnish and allow to dry.

10 Cut four 50mm (2in) lengths from the nails and chamfer the ends to make the stub axles (8). Make the suspension band dowels (7) from 45mm (1¾in) lengths of 6.5mm (¼in) dowel. Hammer the axles and dowels into the suspension arms, as shown.

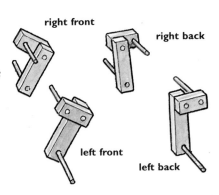

right front

right back

left front

left back

11 Draw four 60mm (2⅜in) diameter circles on the birch plywood, touching the edge, for the wheels (10). Drill a hole in the centre of each wheel with a 6.5mm (¼in) bit. Cut out wheels with the hole saw, sand, varnish and allow to dry.

12 Make four stub axle spacers (9) from 16mm (⅝in) lengths of 12mm (½in) birch dowel. Drill a hole through the centre of the axle spacers and wheel retainers (11) with a 6.5mm (¼in) bit. Varnish the spacers and allow to dry. Paint the wheel retainers black.

13 Fix the wheels and spacers to the stub axles of the suspension arms, making sure that the wheels spin freely. Glue the retainers to the ends of the axles. Slot a scrap of thin card between the retainer and the wheel to prevent the glue from coming into contact with the wheel. Lightly oil the axles.

14 Cut four 12mm (½in) wide bands (15) from the bicycle inner tube and place each band over the suspension band dowels (7). Then insert the dowels through the holes in the chassis, as shown, looping the bands over the protruding ends of the chassis band dowels (2). Make sure that you place the suspension arms in the correct positions.

15 Paint the number plate, using red numbers on a white background, and varnish. When dry, nail it to the back of the chassis with two 25mm (1in) panel pins. Drill the hole shown in the clamp (12), and varnish.

MAKING THE CAB

16 Countersink a 3.2mm (⅛in) hole on both sides of the winch cord guide (34). Shape one side as shown, to prevent the cord chafing. Drill the holes in the beam (19). Position the winch cord guide at the undrilled (front) end of the beam and use a rasp to round the beam flush with the cord guide. Separate the parts, paint the beam black and varnish the cord guide. When dry, nail both pieces together with cut-down panel pins.

17 Cut a 22mm (⅞in) length of 6.5mm (¼in) birch dowel for the tow bar (35). Glue this into the hole in the end of the beam, pointing upwards and flush with the underside.

18 Cut the battery recess hole in the floor (16) with a fretsaw and drill the hole. Glue and nail the beam along the centre of the floor, so that the measurement from the front of the winch cord guide to the front of the floor is 64mm (2½in).

19 Glue the skirts (18) to the underside of the side pieces (17) in the position indicated on the template guide.

20 Glue and nail the sides and skirts to the floor so that the distance from the curved front of the sides to the front of the floor is 45mm (1¾in). The undersides of the floor and sides should be flush. Make sure that the side with the extra hole (see template) is on the right. Glue the pick-up front and back (25) between the sides, resting on the floor. The distance between the pick-up front and the back of the floor should be 140mm (5½in).

21 Paint the sides, skirts and pick-up back green. Leave the edges unpainted. Varnish the whole assembly.

22 Make a recess in the underside of the cab base (20) in the position shown, by cutting through the first layer of ply with a craft knife and chiselling away the excess. Place the nut from the roofing bolt in the recessed hole in the top of the cab base. This must be a tight fit; if it is loose, secure with rapid-drying epoxy glue.

23 Drill a recessed hole for the light switch in one of the cab window frames (21) as shown. This piece becomes the left frame.

24 Glue the window frames to the cab base. Secure with cut-down panel pins hammered through the base into the frames, as shown. Varnish this assembly.

25 Cut a 64 × 100mm (2½ × 4in) rectangle of perspex for the windscreen (23) and use a metal file to chamfer the long sides to an angle of 40°. Drill two holes with a 1.5mm (¹⁄₁₆in) bit on either side of the bottom edge, as shown, and nail it with panel pins to the window frames.

26 Chamfer the bonnet (24) and the front of the cab roof (22), as shown. Drill the recessed hole for the LED in the underside of the cab roof. Paint the bonnet (top and front) and roof (top, sides, front and back) green, and then varnish and allow to dry.

27 Secure the assembly with panel pins. Working from underneath, nail the bonnet to the cab base, close up to the windscreen. Glue and nail the cab roof to the cab window frames.

MAKING THE WINCH

28 Cut a 165mm (6½in) length of 12mm (½in) birch dowel for the winch shaft (26) and round off the ends with glasspaper. Drill a recessed hole in its centre as shown. Varnish and allow to dry.

29 Cut the winch pawl handle (30) and winch pawl shaft (31) from 6.5mm (¼in) birch dowel to lengths of 25mm (1in) and 30mm (1¼in) respectively. Ease out the hole in the winch pawl (29) with a round file so that the shaft turns easily inside it. Drill a second hole in one side of the winch pawl with a 6.5mm (¼in) bit to a depth of 6.5mm (¼in) and glue the handle into this hole. Varnish this assembly and the following parts: winch ratchet (27); winch end (28) and winch hook (33). Allow to dry.

31 Thread the winch cord (32) through the winch cord guide and through the hole in the winch shaft. Knot at the shaft end and seal by melting the cord end with a lighted match. Thread the free end through the hole in the winch hook and knot on both sides to secure. Seal the end as before.

32 Position the winch pawl assembly in the recess in the right side of the bonnet so that the hole for the shaft aligns with the hole in the right side piece. Hammer the winch pawl shaft through the hole, making sure that it locates in the hole in the winch pawl. Check that the winch works satisfactorily. Sand the exposed end of the shaft flush with the side and touch up the paint and varnish.

30 Put the winch shaft through the holes in the cab sides, making sure that it rotates freely. Thread the winch end and ratchet onto the shaft on either side of the central hole, as shown. These should be a tight but movable fit. Centre the shaft between the sides and adjust the position of the winch end and rachet so that there is 1.5mm (¹⁄₁₆in) clearance between them and the sides. Secure with panel pins.

black –
red +

battery

33 For the light holder (37), cut a 6.5mm (¼in) length of 12mm (½in) birch dowel and drill two holes through the centre with a 1.5mm (¹⁄₁₆in) bit. Put the LED (36) in the holder, thread the two wires through the holes and mark the hole through which the longer wire passes as positive (+). Trim both wires to 6.5mm (¼in) and bend up flat. Mount the light and holder in the roof, with the positive (+) wire pointing towards the back of the cab.

34 Insert the switch (38) into the hole in the left window frame. Mark 25mm (1in) along the wires from the battery connector. Thread the free ends of the wire through the hole in the cab base until the marked point is level with the switch tags and cut the red (+) wire only at this point. Solder the bared ends of the red wire to each of the protruding switch tags. Feed the black wire between the tags. Take both wires up the side of the window frame and across the cab roof, and cut them where they meet the LED wires. Bare the ends and solder to the wires, taking care to attach the red wire to the wire marked +. Connect the battery and test. The light should flash when you press the switch.

36 Refer to the exploded diagram and assemble the vehicle. Insert the bolt (13) upwards through the hole in the clamp and position between the beams. Put the body on the chassis so that the bolt passes through the hole in the beam. Put the plugged-in battery in the recess in the body floor. Place the cab assembly on the body, with the bolt passing up through the cab floor. Screw the bolt firmly into the nut to complete the assembly.

35 Staple the wires to the inside of the cab with bent dressmaker's pins.

· INDEX ·